Diabetic Renal Diet Cookbook for Seniors

Over 1500 Days of Delicious Recipes Low in Salt, Sugar, Potassium, and Phosphorus for Diabetes and Kidney Disorder Prevention and Management

Kathleen H. Jensen

CONTENTS

Introduction

Understanding Diabetic Renal Diets

Diabetes and kidney disease are commonly associated, so individuals with both conditions must manage their diet effectively. The chapter "**Understanding Diabetic Renal Diets**" is an integral part of this cookbook. It offers vital knowledge necessary to understand the complexities of a diabetic renal diet, providing insights into critical aspects of this dietary approach. By understanding what a diabetic renal diet entails, you can make informed choices that contribute to managing diabetes and kidney health.

What is a Diabetic Renal Diet?

A diabetic renal diet, also called a kidney-friendly diabetic diet, is a special eating plan for people with diabetes and kidney disease. This diet focuses on finding the right balance to control blood sugar levels and support kidney function. People who have diabetes are more likely to have kidney problems. This diet aims to reduce the stress on the kidneys caused by complications from diabetes.

The key to a diabetic renal diet is moderation. It primarily focuses on regulating the intake of specific nutrients, such as sodium, potassium, and phosphorus. These nutrients can have a significant impact on kidney function and electrolyte balance. Dietary choices are essential for managing kidney damage and maintaining stable blood sugar levels.

Why Prioritize Kidney Health as a Diabetic?

It is crucial for individuals with diabetes and kidney disease to recognize the significance of following a diabetic renal diet for maintaining kidney health. The kidneys are responsible for filtering waste and excess fluids from the blood. When kidney function is impaired, waste products build up in the body. This can result in various health problems, such as high blood pressure, cardiovascular issues, and fluid imbalance. Diabetes can worsen these issues, leading to damage in the kidneys' small blood vessels.

A diabetic renal diet is important because it can help lessen the strain on the kidneys. This diet helps support kidney function and regulate blood sugar levels by managing nutrient intake and balancing electrolytes. This proactive approach may help slow the progression of kidney disease and reduce the risk of further complications, such as the need for dialysis.

Chapter 1

Guidelines for a Renal Diet

To successfully follow a diabetic renal diet, individuals should adhere to specific guidelines and principles:

1. Limit Sodium Intake: High sodium intake can contribute to fluid retention and high blood pressure, which can negatively impact kidney health. Reducing sodium intake is essential, and one way to do this is by selecting low-sodium or sodium-free ingredients and avoiding processed foods high in salt.

2. Monitor Protein Intake: Protein is essential for the body, but excessive protein intake can strain the kidneys. People with kidney disease are commonly recommended to moderate their protein consumption. However, it is equally important to ensure that the protein sources consumed are of high quality, such as lean meats and poultry.

3. Control Phosphorus and Potassium: Elevated levels of phosphorus and potassium can have a negative impact on kidney function. Choose foods with lower amounts of phosphorus and potassium to manage mineral levels. Additionally, taking phosphate binders as prescribed by a healthcare provider may be necessary.

4. Choose Low Glycemic Index (GI) Foods: Selecting low glycemic index (GI) foods is vital for individuals with diabetes to maintain stable blood sugar levels. Foods with a lower GI release glucose more slowly, which helps avoid sudden spikes in blood sugar levels.

5. Balance Fluid Intake: Proper fluid balance is crucial for maintaining kidney health. People with kidney disease may be advised to restrict their fluid intake. Still, the amount should be tailored to their unique requirements, taking into account their stage of kidney disease and other relevant health considerations.

6. Consult with Healthcare Professionals: It is necessary to collaborate with healthcare providers and dietitians who can create a personalized diabetic renal diet plan based on individual needs. Regular monitoring and adjustments are crucial for effectively managing both diabetes and kidney health.

Understanding the basics of a diabetic renal diet is vital for making informed dietary choices, which can improve health outcomes for individuals with diabetes and kidney disease. This chapter sets the groundwork for the rest of the cookbook. In the preceding chapters, you will find various tasty recipes specifically created to meet the dietary needs of individuals with diabetes and kidney disease. These recipes aim to satisfy the taste buds while adhering to the dietary restrictions of a diabetic renal diet.

BREAKFAST

Spinach and Feta Egg White Omelet

Prep Time: 10 minutes
Cook Time: 10 minutes
Number of Servings: 2

Ingredients:

- 1 cup of fresh spinach, chopped
- 1/4 cup of feta cheese, crumbled
- 1/2 cup of egg whites (about 4 large egg whites)
- 1/4 cup of diced tomatoes
- 1/4 cup of diced onions
- 1 clove of garlic, minced
- 1/4 teaspoon of black pepper
- 1/4 teaspoon of olive oil
- Cooking spray (for the pan)

Instructions:

1. Heat the olive oil in a non-stick skillet over medium heat.
2. Add the minced garlic and diced onions to the skillet and sauté for 2 minutes or until the onions become translucent.
3. Add the chopped spinach and diced tomatoes to the skillet. Sauté for an extra 2 minutes or until the spinach wilts.
4. In a separate bowl, whisk the egg whites until frothy.
5. Pour the whisked egg whites into the skillet with the sautéed vegetables. Let the eggs cook undisturbed for about 2-3 minutes, or until they start to set around the edges.
6. Sprinkle the crumbled feta cheese evenly over one-half of the omelet.
7. Using a spatula, carefully fold the other half of the omelet over the cheese side, creating a half-moon shape.

8. Cook for an extra 2 minutes, or until the cheese melts and the omelet is fully properly cooked.

9. Season with black pepper to taste.

10. Carefully transfer the omelet to a plate and serve hot.

Nutritional Information (Per Serving):

- Carbs: 4 grams

- Phosphorus: 100 mg

- Potassium: 250 mg

- Sodium: 350 mg

- Protein: 15 grams

Quinoa Porridge with Blueberries
Prep Time: 5 minutes
Cook Time: 15 minutes
Number of Servings: 2

Ingredients:

- 1/2 cup of quinoa

- 1 1/2 cups of unsweetened almond milk

- 1/4 teaspoon of ground cinnamon

- 1/4 teaspoon of vanilla extract

- 1/2 cup of fresh blueberries

- 1 tablespoon of chopped walnuts (optional)

- 1 tablespoon of honey (optional)

- Cooking spray (for the pot)

Instructions:

1. Rinse the quinoa thoroughly under cold water in a fine-mesh sieve.

2. In a medium-sized pot, spray some cooking spray and add the rinsed quinoa.

3. Toast the quinoa over medium heat for about 2 minutes, stirring occasionally, until it becomes slightly fragrant.

4. Add the unsweetened almond milk to the pot and bring it to a boil over medium-high heat.

5. Once it reaches a boil, reduce the heat to low, cover the pot, and simmer for 12-15 minutes, or until the quinoa is tender and has absorbed most of the almond milk.

6. Stir in the ground cinnamon and vanilla extract.

7. Divide the quinoa porridge between two serving bowls.

8. Top each serving with fresh blueberries and chopped walnuts if desired.

9. Drizzle 1/2 tablespoon of honey over each serving if you prefer extra sweetness (optional).

10. Serve hot and enjoy!

Nutritional Information (Per Serving):

- Carbs: 35 grams

- Phosphorus: 150 mg

- Potassium: 200 mg

- Sodium: 70 mg

- Protein: 7 grams

Scrambled Tofu with Tomatoes and Herbs

Prep Time: 10 minutes
Cook Time: 15 minutes
Number of Servings: 2

Ingredients:

- 1 cup of firm tofu, crumbled

- 1/2 cup of diced tomatoes

- 1/4 cup of diced onions

- 1 clove of garlic, minced

- 1/2 teaspoon of olive oil
- 1/2 teaspoon of dried basil
- 1/2 teaspoon of dried oregano
- 1/4 teaspoon of black pepper
- Cooking spray (for the pan)

Instructions:

1. Heat the olive oil in a non-stick skillet over medium heat.

2. Add the minced garlic and diced onions to the skillet and sauté for 2 minutes or until the onions become translucent.

3. Add the crumbled tofu to the skillet and cook for about 5 minutes, stirring occasionally, until it starts to brown slightly.

4. Stir in the diced tomatoes and keep on cooking for an extra 2 minutes until the tomatoes soften.

5. Sprinkle the dried basil, dried oregano, and black pepper over the tofu and tomato mixture. Stir sufficiently to incorporate the herbs evenly.

6. Cook for an extra 5 minutes, or until the tofu is heated through and has absorbed the flavors of the herbs and tomatoes.

7. Divide the scrambled tofu mixture between two serving plates.

8. Serve hot as a delicious, protein-packed breakfast or brunch option.

Nutritional Information (Per Serving):

- Carbs: 8 grams
- Phosphorus: 150 mg
- Potassium: 250 mg
- Sodium: 60 mg
- Protein: 10 grams

Greek Yogurt Parfait with Almonds and Berries

Prep Time: 10 minutes
Cook Time: 0 minutes
Number of Servings: 2

Ingredients:

- 1 cup of low-fat Greek yogurt
- 1/4 cup of sliced almonds
- 1/2 cup of mixed berries (e.g., strawberries, blueberries, raspberries)
- 1 tablespoon of honey (optional, for drizzling)
- 1/4 teaspoon of cinnamon
- 1/4 teaspoon of vanilla extract

Instructions:

1. In a small bowl, add the low-fat Greek yogurt, vanilla extract, and cinnamon. Mix sufficiently to incorporate the vanilla and cinnamon flavors into the yogurt.

2. In two serving glasses or bowls, begin by adding a layer of the Greek yogurt mixture to the bottom.

3. Next, add a layer of mixed berries on top of the yogurt.

4. Sprinkle a portion of sliced almonds over the berries.

5. Repeat the layering process by adding an extra layer of yogurt, followed by berries and almonds until you've used all the ingredients.

6. If desired, drizzle 1/2 tablespoon of honey over each parfait for extra sweetness (optional).

7. Serve immediately as a healthy and delicious breakfast or snack.

Nutritional Information (Per Serving):

- Carbs: 20 grams
- Phosphorus: 150 mg
- Potassium: 250 mg
- Sodium: 70 mg

- Protein: 12 grams

Veggie and Cheese Breakfast Burrito
Prep Time: 10 minutes
Cook Time: 10 minutes
Number of Servings: 2

Ingredients:

- 2 large eggs
- 1/4 cup of diced red bell pepper
- 1/4 cup of diced green bell pepper
- 1/4 cup of diced onions
- 1/4 cup of shredded low-sodium cheddar cheese
- 2 whole wheat tortillas (8-inch size)
- 1/4 teaspoon of black pepper
- 1/4 teaspoon of olive oil
- Cooking spray (for the pan)

Instructions:

1. Heat the olive oil in a non-stick skillet over medium heat.
2. Add the diced onions, red bell pepper, and green bell pepper to the skillet. Sauté for 2-3 minutes, or until the vegetables become tender.
3. In a small bowl, beat the eggs and black pepper together.
4. Push the sautéed vegetables to one side of the skillet and pour the beaten eggs into the empty side.
5. Scramble the eggs until properly cooked and then mix them with the sautéed vegetables.
6. Warm the whole wheat tortillas in the microwave or on a dry skillet for about 10 seconds to make them pliable.
7. Divide the scrambled egg and vegetable mixture evenly between the two tortillas.

8. Sprinkle two tablespoons of shredded low-sodium cheddar cheese over each burrito.

9. Fold in the sides of the tortillas and then roll them up tightly to create the burritos.

10. Heat a clean skillet over medium heat and coat it with cooking spray.

11. Place the burritos seam-side down on the skillet and cook for 2-3 minutes on each side, or until golden brown and the cheese has melted.

12. Take out the burritos from the skillet, let them cool slightly, and then slice them in half.

13. Serve your veggie and cheese breakfast burritos warm and enjoy!

Nutritional Information (Per Serving):

- Carbs: 30 grams

- Phosphorus: 150 mg

- Potassium: 250 mg

- Sodium: 200 mg

- Protein: 16 grams

Zucchini and Mushroom Frittata
Prep Time: 10 minutes
Cook Time: 20 minutes
Number of Servings: 4

Ingredients:

- 4 large eggs

- 2 cups of sliced zucchini

- 1 cup of sliced mushrooms

- 1/2 cup of diced onions

- 1/4 cup of low-sodium feta cheese, crumbled

- 1/4 cup of fresh basil leaves, chopped

- 1/4 teaspoon of black pepper
- 1/4 teaspoon of olive oil
- Cooking spray (for the pan)

Instructions:

1. Turn on your oven and set it to 350°F (175°C).

2. Heat the olive oil in an oven-safe skillet over medium heat.

3. Add the diced onions and sliced mushrooms to the skillet. Sauté for 2-3 minutes, or until the onions become translucent and the mushrooms start to release their moisture.

4. Add the sliced zucchini to the skillet and continue to sauté for an extra 2-3 minutes, or until the zucchini becomes tender.

5. In a bowl, beat the eggs and black pepper together.

6. Pour the beaten eggs over the sautéed vegetables in the skillet.

7. Sprinkle the crumbled low-sodium feta cheese evenly over the eggs.

8. Cook for 2-3 minutes, or until the edges of the frittata start to set.

9. Transfer the skillet to the preheated oven and bake for 10-12 minutes, or until the frittata is fully set and slightly golden on top.

10. Take out the skillet from the oven and sprinkle the chopped fresh basil over the frittata.

11. Let it cool slightly, then slice the frittata into four equal portions.

12. Serve your zucchini and mushroom frittata warm or at room temperature.

Nutritional Information (Per Serving):

- Carbs: 6 grams
- Phosphorus: 120 mg
- Potassium: 250 mg
- Sodium: 150 mg
- Protein: 9 grams

Cinnamon Raisin Oatmeal with Chia Seeds

Prep Time: 5 minutes
Cook Time: 10 minutes
Number of Servings: 2

Ingredients:

- 1 cup of old-fashioned oats
- 2 cups of water
- 2 tablespoons of chia seeds
- 1/4 cup of raisins
- 1/2 teaspoon of ground cinnamon
- 1/4 teaspoon of vanilla extract
- 1 tablespoon of honey (optional)
- Cooking spray (for the pot)

Instructions:

1. In a medium-sized pot, bring two cups of water to a boil.
2. Stir in the old-fashioned oats and reduce the heat to low.
3. Simmer the oats for about 5-7 minutes, stirring occasionally, until they reach your desired level of thickness.
4. Stir in the chia seeds, raisins, ground cinnamon, and vanilla extract.
5. Keep on cooking for an extra 2-3 minutes, or until the chia seeds have absorbed some of the liquid and the oatmeal is well combined.
6. Take out the pot from the heat.
7. If desired, drizzle 1/2 tablespoon of honey over each serving for extra sweetness (optional).
8. Serve your cinnamon raisin oatmeal with chia seeds warm and enjoy!

Nutritional Information (Per Serving):

- Carbs: 45 grams
- Phosphorus: 150 mg

- Potassium: 200 mg

- Sodium: 10 mg

- Protein: 7 grams

Smoked Salmon and Cream Cheese Wrap

Prep Time: 10 minutes
Cook Time: 0 minutes
Number of Servings: 2

Ingredients:

- 4 ounces of smoked salmon

- 4 tablespoons of low-fat cream cheese

- 2 whole wheat tortillas (8-inch size)

- 1/4 cup of diced red onions

- 1/4 cup of diced cucumbers

- 1 tablespoon of fresh dill, chopped

- 1/4 teaspoon of black pepper

- Cooking spray (for the pan)

Instructions:

1. Lay out the two whole wheat tortillas on a clean surface.

2. Spread two tablespoons of low-fat cream cheese evenly onto each tortilla, leaving a small border around the edges.

3. Divide the smoked salmon equally between the two tortillas, placing it on top of the cream cheese.

4. Sprinkle the diced red onions, diced cucumbers, and chopped fresh dill over the smoked salmon.

5. Season with a pinch of black pepper to taste.

6. Carefully fold in the sides of each tortilla and then roll them up tightly to create the wraps.

7. Heat a clean skillet over medium heat and coat it with cooking spray.

8. Place the wraps seam-side down on the skillet and cook for about 1-2 minutes on each side, or until slightly crispy and the cream cheese has softened.

9. Take out the wraps from the skillet, let them cool slightly, and then slice them in half.

10. Serve your smoked salmon and cream cheese wraps as a delicious and satisfying meal.

Nutritional Information (Per Serving):

- Carbs: 24 grams

- Phosphorus: 200 mg

- Potassium: 250 mg

- Sodium: 500 mg

- Protein: 15 grams

Sweet Potato and Black Bean Breakfast Bowl

Prep Time: 10 minutes
Cook Time: 25 minutes
Number of Servings: 2

Ingredients:

- 1 medium sweet potato, peeled and diced into small cubes

- 1/2 cup of cooked black beans (canned, drained, and rinsed)

- 2 large eggs

- 1/4 cup of diced red bell pepper

- 1/4 cup of diced green bell pepper

- 1/4 cup of diced onions

- 1/4 teaspoon of olive oil

- 1/4 teaspoon of ground cumin

- 1/4 teaspoon of paprika

- 1/4 teaspoon of black pepper

- Cooking spray (for the pan)

Instructions:

1. Turn on your oven and set it to 400°F (200°C).

2. Place the diced sweet potato on a baking sheet lined with parchment paper. Drizzle with olive oil and sprinkle with ground cumin, paprika, and black pepper. Toss to coat the sweet potato cubes evenly with the spices and oil.

3. Roast the sweet potato cubes in the preheated oven for approximately 20-25 minutes, or until tender and slightly crispy, stirring halfway through.

4. While the sweet potatoes are roasting, heat a non-stick skillet over medium heat and coat it with cooking spray.

5. Add the diced onions, red bell pepper, and green bell pepper to the skillet. Sauté for 2-3 minutes, or until the vegetables become tender.

6. Add the cooked black beans to the skillet with the sautéed vegetables and cook for an extra 2 minutes, or until the beans are heated through.

7. In an extra skillet, cook the two eggs to your desired level of doneness (e.g., fried, scrambled, or poached).

8. To assemble the breakfast bowl, divide the roasted sweet potato cubes between two bowls.

9. Top each bowl with the black bean and vegetable mixture.

10. Place one cooked egg on top of each bowl.

11. Serve your sweet potato and black bean breakfast bowls hot, optionally garnished with fresh herbs or a pinch of salt-free seasoning.

Nutritional Information (Per Serving):

- Carbs: 30 grams
- Phosphorus: 220 mg
- Potassium: 500 mg
- Sodium: 150 mg

- Protein: 15 grams

Cottage Cheese Pancakes with Fresh Fruit

Prep Time: 10 minutes
Cook Time: 10 minutes
Number of Servings: 2

Ingredients:

- 1 cup of low-fat cottage cheese
- 2 large eggs
- 1/4 cup of oat flour
- 1/4 cup of fresh berries (e.g., blueberries, strawberries, raspberries)
- 1/4 teaspoon of vanilla extract
- Cooking spray (for the pan)
- 1 tablespoon of honey (optional, for drizzling)

Instructions:

1. In a blender, add the low-fat cottage cheese, eggs, oat flour, and vanilla extract. Blend until you have a smooth batter.
2. Preheat a non-stick skillet over medium heat and coat it with cooking spray.
3. Pour 1/4 cup of the pancake batter onto the skillet for each pancake. You can make 4 pancakes in total.
4. Cook the pancakes for about 2-3 minutes on each side, or until golden brown and properly cooked.
5. While the pancakes are cooking, rinse and prepare the fresh berries.
6. Once the pancakes are done, transfer them to serving plates.
7. Top each pancake with the fresh berries.
8. If desired, drizzle 1/2 tablespoon of honey over each serving for extra sweetness (optional).
9. Serve your cottage cheese pancakes with fresh fruit and enjoy!

Nutritional Information (Per Serving):

- Carbs: 25 grams

- Phosphorus: 200 mg

- Potassium: 250 mg

- Sodium: 300 mg

- Protein: 20 grams

Cinnamon Apple Quinoa Breakfast Bowl

Prep Time: 10 minutes
Cook Time: 20 minutes
Number of Servings: 2

Ingredients:

- 1 cup of cooked quinoa

- 1 medium apple, diced

- 1/4 cup of chopped walnuts

- 1/4 cup of unsweetened almond milk

- 1/2 teaspoon of ground cinnamon

- 1/4 teaspoon of vanilla extract

- 1/4 teaspoon of olive oil

- Cooking spray (for the pan)

- 1 tablespoon of honey (optional, for drizzling)

Instructions:

1. In a non-stick skillet, heat the olive oil over medium heat.

2. Add the diced apple to the skillet and sauté for about 3-4 minutes, or until the apple pieces become slightly tender and start to caramelize.

3. Stir in the cooked quinoa, chopped walnuts, ground cinnamon, and vanilla extract. Cook for an extra 2-3 minutes, stirring occasionally, until the quinoa is heated through and well combined with the other ingredients.

4. Pour the unsweetened almond milk over the quinoa mixture. Stir sufficiently and cook for an extra 2 minutes, or until the almond milk is absorbed and the mixture reaches your desired consistency.

5. Take out the skillet from heat.

6. Divide the cinnamon apple quinoa mixture between two serving bowls.

7. If desired, drizzle 1/2 tablespoon of honey over each serving for extra sweetness (optional).

8. Serve your cinnamon apple quinoa breakfast bowls warm and enjoy!

Nutritional Information (Per Serving):

- Carbs: 40 grams

- Phosphorus: 200 mg

- Potassium: 300 mg

- Sodium: 50 mg

- Protein: 7 grams

Smoked Salmon and Avocado Breakfast Wrap
Prep Time: 10 minutes
Cook Time: 0 minutes
Number of Servings: 2

Ingredients:

- 4 ounces of smoked salmon

- 1 ripe avocado, sliced

- 2 whole wheat tortillas (8-inch size)

- 1/4 cup of diced red onions

- 1/4 cup of diced tomatoes

- 1/4 cup of low-fat cream cheese

- 1/4 teaspoon of black pepper

- Cooking spray (for the pan)

Instructions:

1. Lay out the two whole wheat tortillas on a clean surface.

2. Spread two tablespoons of low-fat cream cheese evenly onto each tortilla.

3. Divide the smoked salmon equally between the two tortillas, placing it on top of the cream cheese.

4. Place the sliced avocado on top of the smoked salmon.

5. Sprinkle the diced red onions and diced tomatoes over the avocado.

6. Season with a pinch of black pepper to taste.

7. Carefully fold in the sides of each tortilla and then roll them up tightly to create the wraps.

8. Heat a clean skillet over medium heat and coat it with cooking spray.

9. Place the wraps seam-side down on the skillet and cook for about 1-2 minutes on each side, or until slightly crispy.

10. Take out the wraps from the skillet, let them cool slightly, and then slice them in half.

11. Serve your smoked salmon and avocado breakfast wraps as a delicious and satisfying meal.

Nutritional Information (Per Serving):

- Carbs: 30 grams
- Phosphorus: 200 mg
- Potassium: 400 mg
- Sodium: 500 mg
- Protein: 18 grams

Spinach and Mushroom Breakfast Casserole
Prep Time: 15 minutes
Cook Time: 40 minutes
Number of Servings: 6

Ingredients:

- 6 large eggs
- 2 cups of fresh spinach, chopped
- 1 cup of sliced mushrooms
- 1/2 cup of diced onions
- 1/2 cup of diced red bell pepper
- 1/4 cup of low-fat milk
- 1/4 cup of low-fat shredded cheddar cheese
- 1/4 teaspoon of olive oil
- 1/4 teaspoon of black pepper
- Cooking spray (for the baking dish)

Instructions:

1. Turn on your oven and set it to 350°F (175°C).
2. Heat the olive oil in a non-stick skillet over medium heat.
3. Add the diced onions and sliced mushrooms to the skillet. Sauté for about 3-4 minutes, or until the onions become translucent and the mushrooms start to brown.
4. Stir in the diced red bell pepper and chopped spinach. Continue to sauté for an extra 2-3 minutes, or until the vegetables are tender and the spinach is wilted. Take it out from heat.
5. In a large mixing bowl, beat the eggs, low-fat milk, and black pepper together until well combined.
6. Spray a baking dish with cooking spray to prevent sticking.
7. Spread the sautéed vegetable mixture evenly in the bottom of the baking dish.
8. Pour the egg mixture over the vegetables.
9. Sprinkle the low-fat shredded cheddar cheese on top.
10. Bake in the preheated oven for about 30-35 minutes, or until the casserole is set in the middle and the top is lightly golden brown.

11. Take out the casserole from the oven and let it cool for a few minutes before slicing it into 6 portions.

12. Serve your spinach and mushroom breakfast casserole warm and enjoy!

Nutritional Information (Per Serving):

- Carbs: 5 grams
- Phosphorus: 150 mg
- Potassium: 200 mg
- Sodium: 200 mg
- Protein: 10 grams

Blueberry Almond Chia Pudding

Prep Time: 5 minutes
Cook Time: 0 minutes
Number of Servings: 2

Ingredients:

- 1/2 cup of chia seeds
- 2 cups of unsweetened almond milk
- 1/2 cup of fresh blueberries
- 1/4 cup of sliced almonds
- 1/2 teaspoon of vanilla extract
- 1 tablespoon of honey (optional, for drizzling)
- A pinch of cinnamon (optional)

Instructions:

1. In a mixing bowl, add the chia seeds, unsweetened almond milk, and vanilla extract. Stir sufficiently to ensure the chia seeds are evenly distributed.

2. Cover the bowl and refrigerate the mixture for at least 2 hours or overnight. This allows the chia seeds to absorb the almond milk and create a pudding-like consistency.

3. Once the chia pudding has thickened, give it a good stir to break up any clumps.

4. To serve, divide the chia pudding into two bowls.

5. Top each bowl with fresh blueberries and sliced almonds.

6. If desired, drizzle 1/2 tablespoon of honey over each serving for extra sweetness (optional).

7. You can also sprinkle a pinch of cinnamon over the top for added flavor (optional).

8. Enjoy your blueberry almond chia pudding as a nutritious and satisfying breakfast or snack!

Nutritional Information (Per Serving):

- Carbs: 20 grams

- Phosphorus: 100 mg

- Potassium: 200 mg

- Sodium: 80 mg

- Protein: 7 grams

Veggie Breakfast Quesadilla

Prep Time: 10 minutes
Cook Time: 10 minutes
Number of Servings: 2

Ingredients:

- 2 large eggs

- 2 whole wheat tortillas (8-inch size)

- 1/2 cup of diced red bell pepper

- 1/2 cup of diced green bell pepper

- 1/2 cup of diced onions

- 1/2 cup of diced tomatoes

- 1/2 cup of shredded low-sodium cheddar cheese

- 1/4 teaspoon of olive oil
- Cooking spray (for the pan)

Instructions:

1. Heat the olive oil in a non-stick skillet over medium heat.
2. Add the diced onions, red bell pepper, and green bell pepper to the skillet. Sauté for 2-3 minutes, or until the vegetables become tender.
3. In a small bowl, beat the eggs.
4. Push the sautéed vegetables to one side of the skillet and pour the beaten eggs into the empty side.
5. Scramble the eggs until properly cooked and then mix them with the sautéed vegetables.
6. Warm the whole wheat tortillas in the microwave or on a dry skillet for about 10 seconds to make them pliable.
7. Divide the scrambled egg and vegetable mixture evenly between the two tortillas.
8. Sprinkle 1/4 cup of shredded low-sodium cheddar cheese over each quesadilla.
9. Fold in the sides of the tortillas and then press them down to form a quesadilla shape.
10. Heat a clean skillet over medium heat and coat it with cooking spray.
11. Place the quesadillas in the skillet and cook for 2-3 minutes on each side, or until golden brown and the cheese has melted.
12. Take out the quesadillas from the skillet, let them cool slightly, and then slice them into wedges.
13. Serve your veggie breakfast quesadillas warm and enjoy!

Nutritional Information (Per Serving):

- Carbs: 30 grams
- Phosphorus: 150 mg
- Potassium: 250 mg

- Sodium: 200 mg
- Protein: 15 grams

Tofu Scramble with Sun-Dried Tomatoes
Prep Time: 10 minutes
Cook Time: 15 minutes
Number of Servings: 4

Ingredients:

- 14 ounces of firm tofu, drained and crumbled
- 1/4 cup of sun-dried tomatoes (not in oil), chopped
- 1/4 cup of diced red bell pepper
- 1/4 cup of diced green bell pepper
- 1/4 cup of diced onions
- 2 cloves of garlic, minced
- 1/4 teaspoon of olive oil
- 1/4 teaspoon of ground turmeric
- 1/4 teaspoon of ground cumin
- 1/4 teaspoon of paprika
- A pinch of black salt (kala namak) for an eggy flavor (optional)
- A pinch of black pepper
- Cooking spray (for the pan)

Instructions:

1. Heat the olive oil in a non-stick skillet over medium heat.
2. Add the diced onions, red bell pepper, and green bell pepper to the skillet. Sauté for 2-3 minutes, or until the vegetables become tender.
3. Stir in the minced garlic and cook for an extra 30 seconds, or until fragrant.

4. Add the crumbled tofu to the skillet, along with the ground turmeric, ground cumin, paprika, and a pinch of black pepper. Mix sufficiently to combine all the ingredients.

5. Keep on cooking the tofu mixture for about 5-7 minutes, stirring occasionally, until the tofu is heated through and starts to brown slightly.

6. Stir in the chopped sun-dried tomatoes and cook for an extra 2 minutes.

7. If desired, add a pinch of black salt for an eggy flavor. Be cautious with the black salt as it can be quite strong, so start with a small amount and adjust to your taste.

8. Keep on cooking for an extra 2-3 minutes, or until the tofu scramble reaches your desired level of doneness.

9. Take out the skillet from heat.

10. Serve your tofu scramble with sun-dried tomatoes hot, optionally garnished with fresh herbs or a sprinkle of nutritional yeast.

Nutritional Information (Per Serving):

- Carbs: 5 grams
- Phosphorus: 140 mg
- Potassium: 350 mg
- Sodium: 180 mg
- Protein: 10 grams

Peanut Butter and Banana Overnight Oats

Prep Time: 5 minutes
Cook Time: 0 minutes (overnight soaking)
Number of Servings: 2

Ingredients:

- 1 cup of old-fashioned oats
- 2 cups of unsweetened almond milk
- 2 tablespoons of natural peanut butter (without added sugar or salt)

- 1 large banana, sliced
- 1/4 teaspoon of ground cinnamon
- 1/4 teaspoon of vanilla extract
- 1 tablespoon of honey (optional, for drizzling)
- Cooking spray (for the jars)

Instructions:

1. In a mixing bowl, add the old-fashioned oats and unsweetened almond milk.
2. Stir in the natural peanut butter, ground cinnamon, and vanilla extract. Mix sufficiently to ensure all the ingredients are fully incorporated.
3. Divide the oat mixture evenly into two mason jars or airtight containers.
4. Top each jar with sliced banana, dividing it equally between the jars.
5. If desired, drizzle 1/2 tablespoon of honey over each jar for extra sweetness (optional).
6. Seal the jars with lids and refrigerate them overnight or for at least 4 hours to allow the oats to soak and soften.
7. Before serving, give the overnight oats a good stir to combine all the ingredients.
8. Enjoy your peanut butter and banana overnight oats as a convenient and delicious breakfast!

Nutritional Information (Per Serving):

- Carbs: 45 grams
- Phosphorus: 200 mg
- Potassium: 350 mg
- Sodium: 150 mg
- Protein: 10 grams

LUNCH

Grilled Chicken Salad with Avocado and Lime Vinaigrette

Prep Time: 20 minutes

Cook Time: 15 minutes

Servings: 4

Ingredients:

- 2 boneless, skinless chicken breasts (about 1 pound)
- 8 cups mixed salad greens
- 2 ripe avocados, sliced
- 1 cup cherry tomatoes, halved
- 1/2 red onion, thinly sliced
- 1/4 cup chopped fresh cilantro
- 1 lime, zested and juiced
- 2 tablespoons olive oil
- 1 clove garlic, minced
- Salt and pepper, to taste

Instructions:

1. Preheat your grill or grill pan to medium-high heat.
2. Season the chicken breasts with salt and pepper. Grill the chicken for about 6-8 minutes per side or until properly cooked, with an internal temperature of 165°F (74°C). Take it out from the grill and let it rest for 5 minutes before slicing it into thin strips.
3. In a large salad bowl, add the mixed salad greens, sliced avocados, cherry tomatoes, red onion, and chopped cilantro.
4. In a small bowl, prepare the Lime Vinaigrette by whisking together the lime zest, lime juice, olive oil, minced garlic, salt, and pepper.
5. Drizzle the Lime Vinaigrette over the salad and toss gently to coat all the ingredients evenly.

6. Divide the salad onto four plates and top each with the grilled chicken strips.

Nutritional Information (per serving):

- Carbs: 15g

- Phosphorus: 210mg

- Potassium: 480mg

- Sodium: 220mg

- Protein: 25g

Lentil and Vegetable Soup

Prep Time: 15 minutes

Cook Time: 30 minutes

Servings: 6

Ingredients:

- 1 cup dried green or brown lentils

- 6 cups low-sodium vegetable broth

- 2 carrots, peeled and diced

- 2 celery stalks, diced

- 1 onion, diced

- 2 cloves garlic, minced

- 1 cup diced tomatoes (canned or fresh)

- 1 teaspoon dried thyme

- 1 teaspoon dried rosemary

- 1 bay leaf

- Salt and pepper, to taste

- 2 tablespoons olive oil

- 1 cup chopped spinach or kale

Instructions:

1. Rinse the lentils thoroughly under cold water and drain them.

2. In a large pot, heat the olive oil over medium heat. Add the diced onions, carrots, and celery. Sauté for about 5 minutes or until the vegetables start to soften.

3. Stir in the minced garlic and continue cooking for an extra minute until fragrant.

4. Add the lentils, diced tomatoes, dried thyme, dried rosemary, bay leaf, and low-sodium vegetable broth to the pot. Season with salt and pepper to taste.

5. Bring the soup to a boil, then reduce the heat to low. Cover and simmer for about 20-25 minutes or until the lentils and vegetables are tender.

6. Stir in the chopped spinach or kale and let it simmer for an extra 5 minutes until wilted.

7. Take out the bay leaf from the soup.

8. Serve hot, and if desired, garnish with a sprinkle of fresh herbs or a drizzle of olive oil.

Nutritional Information (per serving):

- Carbs: 30g
- Phosphorus: 200mg
- Potassium: 450mg
- Sodium: 350mg
- Protein: 12g

Tuna Salad Lettuce Wraps

Prep Time: 15 minutes

Cook Time: 0 minutes

Servings: 4

Ingredients:

- 2 cans (5 ounces each) of low-sodium canned tuna, drained
- 1/2 cup diced celery

- 1/4 cup diced red onion
- 1/4 cup diced pickles (low-sodium)
- 2 tablespoons mayonnaise (low-fat, if preferred)
- 1 tablespoon Dijon mustard
- 1 teaspoon lemon juice
- Salt and pepper, to taste
- 8 large lettuce leaves (such as iceberg or butter lettuce)

Instructions:

1. In a mixing bowl, add the drained tuna, diced celery, diced red onion, and diced pickles.
2. In a small bowl, whisk the mayonnaise, Dijon mustard, and lemon juice until well combined.
3. Pour the mayonnaise mixture over the tuna mixture. Mix sufficiently to coat all the ingredients evenly.
4. Season the tuna salad with salt and pepper to taste. Adjust the seasoning as needed.
5. Carefully wash and dry the lettuce leaves, then arrange them on a clean surface.
6. Divide the tuna salad equally among the lettuce leaves, spooning it into the center of each leaf.
7. Fold the sides of the lettuce leaves over the tuna salad, creating a wrap.
8. Serve the tuna salad lettuce wraps immediately.

Nutritional Information (per serving):

- Carbs: 5g
- Phosphorus: 150mg
- Potassium: 350mg
- Sodium: 350mg
- Protein: 18g

Spinach and Strawberry Salad with Balsamic Glaze

Prep Time: 15 minutes

Cook Time: 5 minutes

Servings: 4

Ingredients:

- 8 cups fresh baby spinach leaves
- 2 cups fresh strawberries, hulled and sliced
- 1/4 cup red onion, thinly sliced
- 1/4 cup crumbled feta cheese (low-sodium, if available)
- 1/4 cup chopped walnuts (unsalted)
- 2 tablespoons balsamic vinegar
- 1 tablespoon olive oil
- 1 teaspoon honey (or sugar substitute for a diabetic option)
- Salt and pepper, to taste

Instructions:

1. In a small saucepan over low heat, add the balsamic vinegar and honey (or sugar substitute). Simmer for about 4-5 minutes, or until the mixture thickens slightly. Take it out from heat and let it cool.

2. In a large salad bowl, add the fresh baby spinach leaves, sliced strawberries, thinly sliced red onion, crumbled feta cheese, and chopped walnuts.

3. Drizzle the olive oil over the salad ingredients and season with salt and pepper to taste. Toss gently to combine.

4. Drizzle the cooled balsamic glaze over the salad. Use it sparingly, as it's concentrated in flavor. You can always add more if desired.

5. Toss the salad one more time to distribute the dressing evenly.

6. Serve the Spinach and Strawberry Salad with Balsamic Glaze immediately.

Nutritional Information (per serving):

- Carbs: 12g

- Phosphorus: 75mg
- Potassium: 450mg
- Sodium: 180mg
- Protein: 4g

Cauliflower and Broccoli Rice Bowl with Grilled Shrimp

Prep Time: 20 minutes

Cook Time: 15 minutes

Servings: 4

Ingredients:

- 1 pound large shrimp, peeled and deveined
- 1 small cauliflower head, cut into florets
- 1 small broccoli head, cut into florets
- 2 tablespoons olive oil
- 1 teaspoon garlic powder
- 1 teaspoon onion powder
- 1/2 teaspoon paprika
- Salt and pepper, to taste
- 1/4 cup low-sodium chicken broth
- 2 cups baby spinach leaves
- 1/4 cup grated Parmesan cheese (low-sodium)
- Lemon wedges, for garnish

Instructions:

1. In a large mixing bowl, add the cauliflower florets and broccoli florets. Use a food processor or box grater to rice them into small, rice-like pieces.

2. Heat one tablespoon of olive oil in a large skillet over medium heat. Add the riced cauliflower and broccoli to the skillet. Season with

garlic powder, onion powder, paprika, salt, and pepper. Sauté for about 5-7 minutes until the vegetables are tender.

3. In a separate skillet, heat the remaining one tablespoon of olive oil over medium-high heat. Add the peeled and deveined shrimp to the skillet. Cook for about 2-3 minutes per side until they turn pink and opaque. Take out the shrimp from the skillet and set them aside.

4. In the same skillet used for the shrimp, add the low-sodium chicken broth and deglaze the pan, scraping up any browned bits from the bottom. Let it simmer for about 2 minutes to reduce slightly.

5. To assemble the bowls, start with a base of the cauliflower and broccoli rice mixture. Top it with baby spinach leaves, grilled shrimp, and a drizzle of the reduced chicken broth.

6. Sprinkle each bowl with grated Parmesan cheese and garnish with lemon wedges.

7. Serve the Cauliflower and Broccoli Rice Bowl with Grilled Shrimp immediately.

Nutritional Information (per serving):

- Carbs: 14g

- Phosphorus: 190mg

- Potassium: 470mg

- Sodium: 260mg

- Protein: 25g

Turkey and Veggie Lettuce Wraps

Prep Time: 20 minutes

Cook Time: 10 minutes

Servings: 4

Ingredients:

- 1 pound ground turkey (lean)

- 1 cup red bell pepper, finely diced

- 1 cup zucchini, finely diced
- 1/2 cup carrot, finely grated
- 1/4 cup low-sodium soy sauce
- 2 cloves garlic, minced
- 1 teaspoon ginger, minced
- 1 teaspoon sesame oil
- 1/4 teaspoon red pepper flakes (optional, adjust to taste)
- 8 large lettuce leaves (such as iceberg or butter lettuce)
- 1/4 cup green onions, thinly sliced
- 2 tablespoons chopped cilantro (optional)
- Lime wedges, for garnish

Instructions:

1. In a large skillet over medium-high heat, cook the ground turkey, breaking it into small pieces with a wooden spoon. Cook for about 5-7 minutes or until it's no longer pink.

2. Add the diced red bell pepper, diced zucchini, and finely grated carrot to the skillet with the turkey. Stir-fry for an extra 3-4 minutes or until the vegetables start to soften.

3. In a small bowl, add the low-sodium soy sauce, minced garlic, minced ginger, sesame oil, and red pepper flakes (if using). Mix sufficiently.

4. Pour the sauce mixture over the turkey and vegetables in the skillet. Stir to coat evenly. Cook for an extra 2 minutes, allowing the flavors to meld.

5. Carefully wash and dry the lettuce leaves, then arrange them on a clean surface.

6. Spoon the turkey and veggie mixture into the center of each lettuce leaf.

7. Garnish with sliced green onions and chopped cilantro (if desired).

8. Serve the Turkey and Veggie Lettuce Wraps with lime wedges on the side for squeezing over the wraps.

Nutritional Information (per serving):

- Carbs: 8g

- Phosphorus: 200mg

- Potassium: 350mg

- Sodium: 360mg

- Protein: 24g

Quinoa and Black Bean Stuffed Bell Peppers

Prep Time: 20 minutes

Cook Time: 40 minutes

Servings: 4

Ingredients:

- 4 large bell peppers (any color)

- 1 cup quinoa, rinsed and drained

- 2 cups low-sodium vegetable broth

- 1 can (15 ounces) black beans, drained and rinsed (low-sodium)

- 1 cup diced tomatoes (canned or fresh)

- 1 cup corn kernels (fresh or frozen)

- 1/2 cup diced red onion

- 1 teaspoon chili powder

- 1/2 teaspoon cumin

- Salt and pepper, to taste

- 1/2 cup shredded low-sodium cheese (optional)

- Fresh cilantro, for garnish (optional)

Instructions:

1. Turn on your oven and set it to 375°F (190°C).

2. Cut the tops off the bell peppers and take out the seeds and membranes. Set aside.

DIABETIC RENAL DIET COOKBOOK FOR SENIORS

3. In a medium saucepan, add the quinoa and low-sodium vegetable broth. Bring to a boil, then reduce the heat to low, cover, and simmer for 15-20 minutes, or until the quinoa is cooked and the liquid is absorbed.

4. In a large mixing bowl, add the cooked quinoa, black beans, diced tomatoes, corn kernels, diced red onion, chili powder, cumin, salt, and pepper. Mix sufficiently.

5. Carefully stuff each bell pepper with the quinoa and black bean mixture, pressing it down gently to pack it.

6. Place the stuffed bell peppers in a baking dish. If desired, sprinkle the shredded low-sodium cheese over the tops of the stuffed peppers.

7. Cover the baking dish with foil and bake in the preheated oven for 25-30 minutes, or until the bell peppers are tender.

8. If using cheese, take out the foil and bake for an extra 5-10 minutes, or until the cheese is melted and bubbly.

9. Garnish the Quinoa and Black Bean Stuffed Bell Peppers with fresh cilantro (if desired) and serve hot.

Nutritional Information (per serving):

- Carbs: 45g

- Phosphorus: 230mg

- Potassium: 680mg

- Sodium: 220mg

- Protein: 14g

Chickpea and Spinach Curry

Prep Time: 15 minutes

Cook Time: 25 minutes

Servings: 4

Ingredients:

- 2 tablespoons olive oil

- 1 large onion, finely chopped
- 3 cloves garlic, minced
- 1-inch piece of fresh ginger, minced
- 1 tablespoon curry powder
- 1 teaspoon ground cumin
- 1 teaspoon ground coriander
- 1/2 teaspoon turmeric
- 1/2 teaspoon paprika
- 1 can (15 ounces) chickpeas, drained and rinsed (low-sodium)
- 1 can (14 ounces) diced tomatoes (low-sodium)
- 1 can (14 ounces) coconut milk (light, if preferred)
- 8 cups fresh spinach leaves
- Salt and pepper, to taste
- Fresh cilantro, for garnish (optional)
- Lemon wedges, for garnish (optional)

Instructions:

1. In a large skillet or pan, heat the olive oil over medium heat. Add the finely chopped onion and sauté for about 5 minutes, or until it becomes translucent.

2. Add the minced garlic and ginger to the skillet. Sauté for an extra 1-2 minutes until fragrant.

3. Stir in the curry powder, ground cumin, ground coriander, turmeric, and paprika. Cook for 1-2 minutes to toast the spices.

4. Add the drained and rinsed chickpeas to the skillet, followed by the diced tomatoes (with their juice). Stir sufficiently to combine.

5. Pour in the coconut milk and mix until everything is evenly combined. Let the mixture simmer for about 10-15 minutes, allowing it to thicken slightly.

6. Add the fresh spinach leaves to the skillet. Stir them into the curry and cook until they wilt and become tender.

7. Season the Chickpea and Spinach Curry with salt and pepper to taste. Adjust the seasoning as needed.

8. Garnish the curry with fresh cilantro and serve hot with lemon wedges on the side (if desired).

Nutritional Information (per serving):

- Carbs: 25g

- Phosphorus: 220mg

- Potassium: 650mg

- Sodium: 220mg

- Protein: 10g

Cucumber and Dill Tuna Salad

Prep Time: 15 minutes

Cook Time: 0 minutes

Servings: 4

Ingredients:

- 2 cans (5 ounces each) of low-sodium canned tuna, drained

- 1 cucumber, diced

- 1/4 cup red onion, finely chopped

- 1/4 cup fresh dill, chopped

- 1/4 cup plain Greek yogurt (low-fat, if preferred)

- 1 tablespoon olive oil

- 1 tablespoon lemon juice

- Salt and pepper, to taste

Instructions:

1. In a large mixing bowl, add the drained canned tuna, diced cucumber, finely chopped red onion, and chopped fresh dill.

2. In a small bowl, whisk the plain Greek yogurt, olive oil, lemon juice, salt, and pepper.

3. Pour the yogurt dressing over the tuna and vegetable mixture in the large bowl.

4. Gently toss all the ingredients until well combined, ensuring the dressing coats everything evenly.

5. Taste and adjust the seasoning with more salt and pepper if needed.

6. Chill the Cucumber and Dill Tuna Salad in the refrigerator for at least 30 minutes before serving. This allows the flavors to meld.

7. Serve the chilled salad as a side dish or on its own.

Nutritional Information (per serving):

- Carbs: 5g
- Phosphorus: 220mg
- Potassium: 270mg
- Sodium: 220mg
- Protein: 15g

Roasted Vegetable and Barley Salad

Prep Time: 15 minutes

Cook Time: 45 minutes

Servings: 4

Ingredients:

- 1 cup pearl barley
- 2 cups low-sodium vegetable broth
- 2 cups mixed vegetables (such as bell peppers, zucchini, cherry tomatoes, and red onion), chopped into bite-sized pieces
- 2 tablespoons olive oil
- 1 teaspoon dried thyme
- 1 teaspoon dried rosemary
- Salt and pepper, to taste
- 1/4 cup fresh parsley, chopped

- 1/4 cup balsamic vinegar
- 1/4 cup crumbled feta cheese (low-sodium, if available)

Instructions:

1. Turn on your oven and set it to 425°F (220°C).
2. In a medium saucepan, add the pearl barley and low-sodium vegetable broth. Bring to a boil, then reduce the heat to low, cover, and simmer for 30-35 minutes, or until the barley is tender and the liquid is absorbed. Take it out from heat and let it cool.
3. While the barley is cooking, spread the mixed vegetables on a baking sheet. Drizzle with olive oil and sprinkle with dried thyme, dried rosemary, salt, and pepper. Toss to coat the vegetables evenly.
4. Roast the vegetables in the preheated oven for about 15-20 minutes, or until tender and slightly caramelized. Stir them once or twice during roasting for even cooking.
5. In a large mixing bowl, add the cooked barley and roasted vegetables.
6. Add the chopped fresh parsley and balsamic vinegar to the bowl. Toss everything together to combine.
7. Season the Roasted Vegetable and Barley Salad with additional salt and pepper to taste, if needed.
8. Sprinkle the crumbled feta cheese over the salad and gently mix.
9. Serve the salad at room temperature or chilled.

Nutritional Information (per serving):

- Carbs: 45g
- Phosphorus: 200mg
- Potassium: 350mg
- Sodium: 180mg
- Protein: 7g

Roasted Beet and Walnut Salad

Prep Time: 15 minutes

Cook Time: 45 minutes

Servings: 4

Ingredients:

- 4 medium-sized beets, peeled and cut into 1-inch cubes
- 1/2 cup walnuts, chopped
- 4 cups mixed salad greens (such as spinach and arugula)
- 1/4 cup red onion, thinly sliced
- 1/4 cup crumbled goat cheese (low-sodium, if available)
- 2 tablespoons olive oil
- 1 tablespoon balsamic vinegar
- 1 teaspoon honey (or sugar substitute for a diabetic option)
- Salt and pepper, to taste

Instructions:

1. Turn on your oven and set it to 400°F (200°C).
2. Place the cubed beets on a baking sheet. Drizzle with olive oil and season with salt and pepper. Toss to coat the beets evenly.
3. Roast the beets in the preheated oven for about 40-45 minutes, or until tender and can be easily pierced with a fork. Take it out from the oven and let them cool slightly.
4. While the beets are roasting, toast the chopped walnuts in a dry skillet over medium heat for about 3-5 minutes, or until they become fragrant and lightly browned. Set aside.
5. In a small bowl, whisk the balsamic vinegar and honey (or sugar substitute) to create the dressing.
6. In a large salad bowl, add the mixed salad greens, thinly sliced red onion, and roasted beets.
7. Drizzle the dressing over the salad and toss gently to coat all the ingredients.

8. Sprinkle the toasted walnuts and crumbled goat cheese over the salad.

9. Serve the Roasted Beet and Walnut Salad immediately.

Nutritional Information (per serving):

- Carbs: 20g

- Phosphorus: 120mg

- Potassium: 480mg

- Sodium: 220mg

- Protein: 6g

Lemon Garlic Shrimp and Asparagus

Prep Time: 15 minutes

Cook Time: 15 minutes

Servings: 4

Ingredients:

- 1 pound large shrimp, peeled and deveined

- 1 bunch fresh asparagus, trimmed and cut into 2-inch pieces

- 4 cloves garlic, minced

- Zest and juice of 1 lemon

- 2 tablespoons olive oil

- 1 tablespoon fresh parsley, chopped

- Salt and pepper, to taste

- Lemon wedges, for garnish (optional)

Instructions:

1. In a large bowl, add the peeled and deveined shrimp with the minced garlic, lemon zest, and one tablespoon of olive oil. Toss to coat the shrimp evenly. Let it marinate for about 10 minutes.

2. Heat a large skillet or pan over medium-high heat. Add the marinated shrimp and cook for 1-2 minutes per side until they turn

pink and opaque. Take out the cooked shrimp from the skillet and set them aside.

3. In the same skillet, add the remaining one tablespoon of olive oil. Add the trimmed asparagus pieces and sauté for about 5-7 minutes until they become tender-crisp and slightly charred.

4. Return the cooked shrimp to the skillet with the asparagus.

5. Drizzle the lemon juice over the shrimp and asparagus in the skillet. Season with salt and pepper to taste. Toss everything together to combine and heat through.

6. Garnish the Lemon Garlic Shrimp and Asparagus with chopped fresh parsley and lemon wedges (if desired).

7. Serve hot.

Nutritional Information (per serving):

- Carbs: 7g

- Phosphorus: 160mg

- Potassium: 340mg

- Sodium: 220mg

- Protein: 22g

Mediterranean Chickpea Salad

Prep Time: 15 minutes

Cook Time: 0 minutes

Servings: 4

Ingredients:

- 2 cans (15 ounces each) chickpeas, drained and rinsed (low-sodium)

- 1 cup cucumber, diced

- 1 cup cherry tomatoes, halved

- 1/2 cup red onion, finely chopped

- 1/2 cup Kalamata olives, pitted and sliced

- 1/4 cup fresh parsley, chopped

- 1/4 cup fresh mint leaves, chopped
- 1/4 cup feta cheese, crumbled (low-sodium, if available)
- 2 tablespoons olive oil
- 2 tablespoons lemon juice
- 1 teaspoon dried oregano
- Salt and pepper, to taste

Instructions:

1. In a large salad bowl, add the drained and rinsed chickpeas, diced cucumber, halved cherry tomatoes, finely chopped red onion, sliced Kalamata olives, chopped fresh parsley, and chopped fresh mint leaves.

2. In a small bowl, whisk the olive oil, lemon juice, dried oregano, salt, and pepper to create the dressing.

3. Pour the dressing over the chickpea salad in the large bowl. Toss gently to coat all the ingredients evenly.

4. Sprinkle the crumbled feta cheese over the salad.

5. Taste and adjust the seasoning with more salt and pepper if needed.

6. Chill the Mediterranean Chickpea Salad in the refrigerator for at least 30 minutes before serving. This allows the flavors to meld.

7. Serve the chilled salad as a side dish or on its own.

Nutritional Information (per serving):

- Carbs: 38g
- Phosphorus: 200mg
- Potassium: 440mg
- Sodium: 240mg
- Protein: 14g

Broccoli and Cheddar Stuffed Sweet Potato
Prep Time: 15 minutes

Cook Time: 1 hour

Servings: 4

Ingredients:

- 4 medium-sized sweet potatoes
- 2 cups broccoli florets, steamed and chopped
- 1 cup sharp cheddar cheese, shredded (low-sodium)
- 1/2 cup Greek yogurt (low-fat, if preferred)
- 2 green onions, thinly sliced
- Salt and pepper, to taste
- Fresh parsley, for garnish (optional)

Instructions:

1. Turn on your oven and set it to 400°F (200°C).
2. Scrub the sweet potatoes thoroughly and pierce them several times with a fork. Place them on a baking sheet and bake in the preheated oven for about 45-50 minutes, or until tender and can be easily pierced with a fork.
3. While the sweet potatoes are baking, steam the broccoli florets until tender but still slightly crisp. Chop them into smaller pieces.
4. Once the sweet potatoes are cooked, carefully cut a slit lengthwise down the center of each potato, creating a pocket for the filling.
5. In a bowl, mix the chopped broccoli with 3/4 cup of shredded cheddar cheese, Greek yogurt, sliced green onions, salt, and pepper.
6. Stuff each sweet potato with the broccoli and cheese mixture.
7. Top each stuffed sweet potato with the remaining cheddar cheese.
8. Place the stuffed sweet potatoes back in the oven and bake for an extra 10 minutes, or until the cheese is melted and slightly golden.
9. Garnish with fresh parsley (if desired) and serve hot.

Nutritional Information (per serving):

- Carbs: 43g
- Phosphorus: 230mg

- Potassium: 950mg
- Sodium: 240mg
- Protein: 16g

Turkey and Spinach Stuffed Mushrooms

Prep Time: 20 minutes

Cook Time: 25 minutes

Servings: 4

Ingredients:

- 16 large button mushrooms
- 1/2 pound ground turkey (lean)
- 1 cup fresh spinach, chopped
- 1/4 cup red bell pepper, finely diced
- 1/4 cup onion, finely chopped
- 2 cloves garlic, minced
- 1/4 cup grated Parmesan cheese (low-sodium)
- 2 tablespoons olive oil
- 1/2 teaspoon dried oregano
- Salt and pepper, to taste

Instructions:

1. Turn on your oven and set it to 375°F (190°C).
2. Take out the stems from the mushrooms and finely chop them.
3. In a large skillet, heat the olive oil over medium heat. Add the chopped mushroom stems, finely diced red bell pepper, finely chopped onion, and minced garlic. Sauté for about 5 minutes, or until the vegetables are softened.
4. Add the ground turkey to the skillet. Cook for about 5-7 minutes, breaking it into small pieces with a wooden spoon, until it's no longer pink.

5. Stir in the chopped fresh spinach and cook for an extra 2-3 minutes until it wilts and combines with the turkey mixture.

6. Take out the skillet from the heat and stir in the grated Parmesan cheese and dried oregano. Season with salt and pepper to taste.

7. Carefully stuff each mushroom cap with the turkey and spinach mixture, pressing it down gently to pack it.

8. Place the stuffed mushrooms on a baking sheet.

9. Bake in the preheated oven for about 12-15 minutes, or until the mushrooms are tender and the filling is heated through.

10. Serve the Turkey and Spinach Stuffed Mushrooms hot.

Nutritional Information (per serving):

- Carbs: 8g

- Phosphorus: 180mg

- Potassium: 380mg

- Sodium: 180mg

- Protein: 15g

Grilled Eggplant and Red Pepper Wrap

Prep Time: 15 minutes

Cook Time: 20 minutes

Servings: 4

Ingredients:

- 1 large eggplant, cut into 1/2-inch slices

- 2 red bell peppers, halved and seeded

- 1/4 cup olive oil

- 2 cloves garlic, minced

- 1/4 cup fresh basil leaves

- 1/4 cup fresh parsley leaves

- 2 tablespoons balsamic vinegar

- 4 whole-wheat tortillas (10-inch diameter)

- Salt and pepper, to taste

- 1/2 cup feta cheese, crumbled (low-sodium, if available)

Instructions:

1. Preheat your grill to medium-high heat.

2. Brush the eggplant slices and red bell pepper halves with olive oil. Season them with minced garlic, salt, and pepper.

3. Place the eggplant slices and red bell pepper halves on the grill. Grill for about 5-7 minutes per side, or until tender and have grill marks.

4. While the vegetables are grilling, in a food processor, add the fresh basil, fresh parsley, and balsamic vinegar. Blend until you have a smooth herb sauce.

5. Take out the grilled vegetables from the grill and let them cool slightly.

6. Cut the grilled red bell pepper halves into strips.

7. Lay out the whole-wheat tortillas and spread a portion of the herb sauce on each tortilla.

8. Place a few grilled eggplant slices and some grilled red bell pepper strips on each tortilla.

9. Sprinkle crumbled feta cheese over the vegetables on each tortilla.

10. Fold in the sides of each tortilla and then roll them up, creating a wrap.

11. Serve the Grilled Eggplant and Red Pepper Wraps warm.

Nutritional Information (per serving):

- Carbs: 38g

- Phosphorus: 180mg

- Potassium: 660mg

- Sodium: 320mg

- Protein: 7g

Quinoa and Black Bean Salad with Lime Vinaigrette

Prep Time: 15 minutes

Cook Time: 15 minutes

Servings: 4

Ingredients:

- 1 cup quinoa
- 2 cups water
- 1 can (15 ounces) black beans, drained and rinsed (low-sodium)
- 1 cup corn kernels (fresh or frozen)
- 1 red bell pepper, diced
- 1/2 cup red onion, finely chopped
- 1/4 cup fresh cilantro, chopped
- 2 tablespoons olive oil
- Juice of 2 limes
- 1 teaspoon ground cumin
- Salt and pepper, to taste
- 1/2 cup crumbled queso fresco cheese (low-sodium, if available) for garnish (optional)

Instructions:

1. Rinse the quinoa thoroughly under cold running water in a fine-mesh strainer.
2. In a medium saucepan, add the rinsed quinoa and two cups of water. Bring to a boil over high heat.
3. Reduce the heat to low, cover the saucepan, and simmer for 12-15 minutes, or until the quinoa is cooked and the water is absorbed. Take it out from heat and let it cool.
4. In a large mixing bowl, add the cooked quinoa, drained and rinsed black beans, corn kernels, diced red bell pepper, finely chopped red onion, and chopped fresh cilantro.

5. In a separate small bowl, whisk the olive oil, lime juice, ground cumin, salt, and pepper to create the vinaigrette.

6. Pour the lime vinaigrette over the quinoa and black bean mixture in the large bowl. Toss gently to coat all the ingredients evenly.

7. Taste and adjust the seasoning with more salt and pepper if needed.

8. Chill the Quinoa and Black Bean Salad in the refrigerator for at least 30 minutes before serving. This allows the flavors to meld.

9. Garnish with crumbled queso fresco cheese (if desired) and serve.

Nutritional Information (per serving):

- Carbs: 52g

- Phosphorus: 280mg

- Potassium: 520mg

- Sodium: 220mg

- Protein: 13g

DINNER

Baked Salmon with Lemon and Dill

Prep Time: 15 minutes **Cook Time:** 20 minutes **Servings:** 4

Ingredients:

- 4 salmon fillets (about 6 ounces each)
- 2 lemons, sliced
- 4 sprigs of fresh dill
- 1/4 cup fresh lemon juice
- 2 cloves garlic, minced
- 1/4 cup low-sodium chicken broth
- 1/4 teaspoon black pepper
- 1/4 teaspoon salt

Instructions:

1. Turn on your oven and set it to 375°F (190°C). Place a piece of aluminum foil on a baking sheet and lightly grease it with cooking spray.

2. Arrange the salmon fillets on the prepared baking sheet.

3. Lay two lemon slices on top of each salmon fillet and place a dill sprig on top of the lemon slices.

4. In a small bowl, mix together the fresh lemon juice, minced garlic, low-sodium chicken broth, black pepper, and salt.

5. Pour the lemon juice mixture evenly over the salmon fillets.

6. Seal the aluminum foil around the salmon, creating a packet to keep the moisture in.

7. Bake the salmon in the preheated oven for about 15-20 minutes, or until the salmon flakes easily with a fork.

8. Carefully open the foil packet to release the steam. Serve the salmon hot, garnished with extra dill and lemon slices if desired.

Nutritional Information (per serving):

- Carbs: 3 grams

- Phosphorus: 242 mg

- Potassium: 682 mg

- Sodium: 250 mg

- Protein: 34 grams

Grilled Tofu and Asparagus with Tahini Sauce

Prep Time: 30 minutes **Cook Time:** 10 minutes **Servings:** 4

Ingredients:

- 14 ounces (about 1 block) extra-firm tofu

- 1 bunch of fresh asparagus spears

- 2 tablespoons olive oil

- 1/4 cup tahini

- 2 tablespoons fresh lemon juice

- 2 cloves garlic, minced

- 1/4 teaspoon salt

- 1/4 teaspoon black pepper

- 1 tablespoon chopped fresh parsley (for garnish)

Instructions:

1. Start by preparing the tofu. Place the tofu block on a plate lined with paper towels. Put an extra layer of paper towels on top of the tofu, then place a heavy object, like a cast-iron skillet, on top to press out excess moisture. Let it press for about 15 minutes.

2. While the tofu is pressing, prepare the asparagus. Snap off the tough ends of the asparagus spears and set them aside.

3. In a small bowl, whisk the tahini, fresh lemon juice, minced garlic, salt, and black pepper. Set aside for later use.

4. Preheat your grill to medium-high heat.

5. Cut the pressed tofu into 1/2-inch thick slices.

6. Brush the tofu slices and asparagus spears with olive oil.

7. Place the tofu slices and asparagus on the grill. Grill the tofu for about 3-4 minutes per side, or until grill marks appear and the tofu is heated through. Grill the asparagus for about 2-3 minutes, turning occasionally until tender but still crisp.

8. Take out the grilled tofu and asparagus from the grill.

9. To serve, arrange the grilled tofu and asparagus on a serving platter. Drizzle the tahini sauce over the top, and garnish with chopped fresh parsley.

Nutritional Information (per serving):

- Carbs: 11 grams
- Phosphorus: 113 mg
- Potassium: 397 mg
- Sodium: 168 mg
- Protein: 11 grams

Chicken and Vegetable Stir-Fry with Brown Rice
Prep Time: 15 minutes **Cook Time:** 20 minutes **Servings:** 4

Ingredients:

- 1 cup brown rice
- 2 boneless, skinless chicken breasts (about 1 pound), cut into bite-sized pieces
- 2 cups broccoli florets
- 1 red bell pepper, sliced
- 1 yellow bell pepper, sliced
- 1 small onion, thinly sliced
- 2 cloves garlic, minced
- 2 tablespoons low-sodium soy sauce
- 1 tablespoon olive oil

- 1/2 teaspoon ground ginger
- 1/2 teaspoon black pepper
- 1/4 teaspoon salt
- 1 tablespoon chopped green onions (for garnish)

Instructions:

1. Cook the brown rice according to the package instructions. Set aside and keep warm.

2. In a small bowl, add the low-sodium soy sauce, ground ginger, black pepper, and salt. Mix sufficiently and set aside.

3. Heat the olive oil in a large skillet or wok over medium-high heat.

4. Add the chicken pieces to the skillet and stir-fry for 5-6 minutes, or until no longer pink in the center. Take out the chicken from the skillet and set it aside.

5. In the same skillet, add the minced garlic, sliced onion, broccoli florets, and sliced bell peppers. Stir-fry for 3-4 minutes, or until the vegetables are tender-crisp.

6. Return the cooked chicken to the skillet with the vegetables.

7. Pour the soy sauce mixture over the chicken and vegetables. Stir-fry for an extra 2-3 minutes to coat everything evenly and heat through.

8. To serve, divide the cooked brown rice among four plates. Top each serving with the chicken and vegetable stir-fry mixture.

9. Garnish with chopped green onions.

Nutritional Information (per serving):

- Carbs: 42 grams
- Phosphorus: 285 mg
- Potassium: 562 mg
- Sodium: 416 mg
- Protein: 29 grams

Eggplant and Chickpea Tagine

Prep Time: 20 minutes Cook Time: 40 minutes Servings: 4

Ingredients:

- 1 large eggplant, cubed
- 1 can (15 ounces) chickpeas, drained and rinsed
- 1 onion, finely chopped
- 2 cloves garlic, minced
- 2 tomatoes, diced
- 2 tablespoons olive oil
- 1 teaspoon ground cumin
- 1 teaspoon ground coriander
- 1/2 teaspoon ground cinnamon
- 1/4 teaspoon ground paprika
- 1/4 teaspoon cayenne pepper (adjust to taste)
- 1/4 teaspoon salt
- 1/4 teaspoon black pepper
- 1/2 cup low-sodium vegetable broth
- 2 tablespoons chopped fresh cilantro (for garnish)
- 2 tablespoons chopped fresh parsley (for garnish)

Instructions:

1. In a large skillet, heat the olive oil over medium heat.

2. Add the chopped onion and minced garlic to the skillet. Sauté for about 2-3 minutes until the onion becomes translucent.

3. Add the cubed eggplant to the skillet and continue to sauté for 5-7 minutes, or until the eggplant starts to soften.

4. Stir in the ground cumin, ground coriander, ground cinnamon, ground paprika, cayenne pepper, salt, and black pepper. Cook for an extra 2 minutes to toast the spices, stirring constantly.

5. Add the diced tomatoes and chickpeas to the skillet. Stir sufficiently to combine with the spiced eggplant mixture.

6. Pour in the low-sodium vegetable broth and bring the mixture to a simmer. Reduce the heat to low, cover the skillet, and let it simmer for 20-25 minutes, or until the eggplant is tender and the flavors have melded together. If the mixture becomes too dry, you can add a little more vegetable broth as needed.

7. Once the tagine is ready, garnish with chopped fresh cilantro and parsley.

8. Serve the Eggplant and Chickpea Tagine hot over brown rice or whole wheat couscous.

Nutritional Information (per serving):

- Carbs: 35 grams

- Phosphorus: 189 mg

- Potassium: 594 mg

- Sodium: 275 mg

- Protein: 9 grams

Spaghetti Squash with Turkey Bolognese

Prep Time: 15 minutes **Cook Time:** 50 minutes **Servings:** 4

Ingredients:

- 1 medium-sized spaghetti squash

- 1 pound ground turkey

- 1 small onion, finely chopped

- 2 cloves garlic, minced

- 1 can (15 ounces) crushed tomatoes

- 1/2 cup low-sodium chicken broth

- 1 teaspoon olive oil

- 1/2 teaspoon dried oregano

- 1/2 teaspoon dried basil

- 1/4 teaspoon dried thyme

- 1/4 teaspoon black pepper

- 1/4 teaspoon salt

- 1/4 cup grated Parmesan cheese (optional, for garnish)

- Fresh basil leaves, for garnish

Instructions:

1. Turn on your oven and set it to 375°F (190°C).

2. Cut the spaghetti squash in half lengthwise and scoop out the seeds. Place the squash halves, cut side down, on a baking sheet lined with parchment paper. Bake in the preheated oven for 35-40 minutes or until the squash flesh is tender.

3. While the squash is baking, heat the olive oil in a large skillet over medium heat.

4. Add the chopped onion and minced garlic to the skillet. Sauté for about 2-3 minutes until the onion becomes translucent.

5. Add the ground turkey to the skillet and cook, breaking it apart with a spoon, until it's browned and properly cooked.

6. Stir in the dried oregano, dried basil, dried thyme, black pepper, and salt.

7. Add the crushed tomatoes and low-sodium chicken broth to the skillet. Bring the mixture to a simmer, reduce the heat to low, cover, and let it simmer for 10-15 minutes.

8. Once the spaghetti squash is done baking, use a fork to scrape the flesh into spaghetti-like strands.

9. Serve the spaghetti squash topped with the turkey Bolognese sauce.

10. Garnish with grated Parmesan cheese (if desired) and fresh basil leaves.

Nutritional Information (per serving):

- Carbs: 18 grams

- Phosphorus: 282 mg

- Potassium: 475 mg

- Sodium: 420 mg
- Protein: 27 grams

Cod with Tomato and Olive Tapenade

Prep Time: 15 minutes **Cook Time:** 20 minutes **Servings:** 4

Ingredients:

- 4 cod fillets (about 6 ounces each)
- 1 can (14 ounces) diced tomatoes, drained
- 1/2 cup pitted black olives, chopped
- 2 cloves garlic, minced
- 2 tablespoons fresh basil, chopped
- 1 tablespoon olive oil
- 1/4 teaspoon black pepper
- 1/4 teaspoon salt
- 1/4 teaspoon dried oregano
- 1/4 teaspoon dried thyme
- 1/4 teaspoon red pepper flakes (adjust to taste)
- 1 lemon, sliced (for garnish)

Instructions:

1. Turn on your oven and set it to 375°F (190°C).
2. In a medium-sized bowl, add the drained diced tomatoes, chopped black olives, minced garlic, fresh basil, olive oil, dried oregano, dried thyme, red pepper flakes, salt, and black pepper. Mix sufficiently to make the tomato and olive tapenade.
3. Place the cod fillets in a baking dish large enough to accommodate them in a single layer.
4. Spread the tomato and olive tapenade evenly over the cod fillets.
5. Lay lemon slices on top of the tapenade.
6. Cover the baking dish with foil.

7. Bake in the preheated oven for 15-20 minutes, or until the cod flakes easily with a fork and is properly cooked.

8. Serve the Cod with Tomato and Olive Tapenade hot, garnished with additional fresh basil if desired.

Nutritional Information (per serving):

- Carbs: 8 grams

- Phosphorus: 310 mg

- Potassium: 620 mg

- Sodium: 520 mg

- Protein: 29 grams

Quinoa and Kale Stuffed Peppers
Prep Time: 20 minutes **Cook Time:** 40 minutes **Servings:** 4

Ingredients:

- 4 large bell peppers, any color

- 1 cup quinoa, rinsed and drained

- 2 cups low-sodium vegetable broth

- 2 cups chopped kale, stems removed

- 1 can (15 ounces) low-sodium black beans, drained and rinsed

- 1 cup diced tomatoes (canned or fresh)

- 1/2 cup diced red onion

- 2 cloves garlic, minced

- 1 teaspoon olive oil

- 1/2 teaspoon ground cumin

- 1/2 teaspoon chili powder

- 1/4 teaspoon black pepper

- 1/4 teaspoon salt

- 1/4 cup grated low-sodium Parmesan cheese (optional, for garnish)

Instructions:

1. Turn on your oven and set it to 375°F (190°C).

2. Cut the tops off the bell peppers and take out the seeds and membranes. Set aside.

3. In a medium-sized saucepan, add the quinoa and low-sodium vegetable broth. Bring to a boil, then reduce heat to low, cover, and simmer for 15-20 minutes, or until the quinoa is cooked and the liquid is absorbed.

4. While the quinoa is cooking, heat olive oil in a large skillet over medium heat.

5. Add the minced garlic and diced red onion to the skillet. Sauté for 2-3 minutes until the onion becomes translucent.

6. Stir in the chopped kale, ground cumin, chili powder, black pepper, and salt. Cook for an extra 2-3 minutes until the kale wilts.

7. In a large mixing bowl, add the cooked quinoa, sautéed kale mixture, drained black beans, and diced tomatoes. Mix sufficiently.

8. Stuff each bell pepper with the quinoa and kale mixture.

9. Place the stuffed peppers in a baking dish, and cover with aluminum foil.

10. Bake in the preheated oven for 25-30 minutes, or until the peppers are tender.

11. If desired, sprinkle grated low-sodium Parmesan cheese over the stuffed peppers and return them to the oven for an extra 5 minutes or until the cheese is melted.

12. Serve the Quinoa and Kale Stuffed Peppers hot.

Nutritional Information (per serving):

- Carbs: 53 grams
- Phosphorus: 362 mg
- Potassium: 776 mg
- Sodium: 426 mg
- Protein: 15 grams

Teriyaki Glazed Tempeh with Broccoli

Prep Time: 15 minutes **Cook Time:** 20 minutes **Servings:** 4

Ingredients:

- 1 package (8 ounces) tempeh, cut into cubes
- 4 cups broccoli florets
- 1/2 cup low-sodium teriyaki sauce
- 2 cloves garlic, minced
- 1 tablespoon low-sodium soy sauce
- 1 tablespoon olive oil
- 1/4 teaspoon ground ginger
- 1/4 teaspoon black pepper
- 1/4 teaspoon salt
- 1/4 teaspoon red pepper flakes (adjust to taste)
- 2 green onions, chopped (for garnish)

Instructions:

1. In a small bowl, mix together the low-sodium teriyaki sauce, minced garlic, low-sodium soy sauce, ground ginger, black pepper, salt, and red pepper flakes. Set aside.

2. Heat the olive oil in a large skillet or wok over medium-high heat.

3. Add the cubed tempeh to the skillet and cook for about 5-7 minutes, stirring occasionally, until it begins to brown.

4. Pour the teriyaki sauce mixture over the tempeh in the skillet. Stir sufficiently to coat the tempeh.

5. Add the broccoli florets to the skillet and stir-fry for an extra 5-7 minutes, or until the broccoli is tender-crisp and the sauce has thickened.

6. Serve the Teriyaki Glazed Tempeh with Broccoli hot, garnished with chopped green onions.

Nutritional Information (per serving):

- Carbs: 24 grams

- Phosphorus: 263 mg

- Potassium: 394 mg

- Sodium: 778 mg

- Protein: 16 grams

Turkey and Spinach Meatballs in Tomato Sauce

Prep Time: 20 minutes **Cook Time:** 25 minutes **Servings:** 4

Ingredients:

- 1 pound ground turkey

- 1 cup chopped fresh spinach

- 1/4 cup breadcrumbs

- 1/4 cup grated Parmesan cheese (optional)

- 1/4 cup chopped fresh parsley

- 1/4 cup chopped onion

- 1 egg

- 2 cloves garlic, minced

- 1/4 teaspoon black pepper

- 1/4 teaspoon salt

- 1/4 teaspoon dried oregano

- 1/4 teaspoon dried basil

- 1 can (14 ounces) low-sodium diced tomatoes

- 1/2 cup low-sodium tomato sauce

- 1/4 teaspoon red pepper flakes (optional)

- 1/4 cup shredded low-sodium mozzarella cheese (optional, for garnish)

Instructions:

1. Turn on your oven and set it to 375°F (190°C).

2. In a large mixing bowl, add the ground turkey, chopped fresh spinach, breadcrumbs, grated Parmesan cheese (if using), chopped fresh parsley, chopped onion, egg, minced garlic, black pepper, salt, dried oregano, and dried basil. Mix until all ingredients are well combined.

3. Shape the mixture into meatballs, about 1.5 inches in diameter.

4. Place the meatballs in a baking dish.

5. In a separate bowl, add the low-sodium diced tomatoes, low-sodium tomato sauce, and red pepper flakes (if using). Pour this tomato sauce mixture over the meatballs.

6. Cover the baking dish with aluminum foil.

7. Bake in the preheated oven for 20-25 minutes, or until the meatballs are properly cooked.

8. If desired, sprinkle shredded low-sodium mozzarella cheese over the meatballs and return to the oven for an extra 2-3 minutes or until the cheese is melted and bubbly.

9. Serve the Turkey and Spinach Meatballs in Tomato Sauce hot.

Nutritional Information (per serving):

- Carbs: 13 grams

- Phosphorus: 235 mg

- Potassium: 470 mg

- Sodium: 427 mg

- Protein: 30 grams

Ratatouille with Herbed Quinoa

Prep Time: 20 minutes **Cook Time:** 40 minutes **Servings:** 4

Ingredients:

- 1 eggplant, cut into 1-inch cubes

- 1 zucchini, cut into 1-inch cubes

- 1 yellow bell pepper, cut into 1-inch cubes

- 1 red bell pepper, cut into 1-inch cubes

- 1 onion, chopped

- 2 cloves garlic, minced

- 2 tablespoons olive oil

- 1 can (14 ounces) low-sodium diced tomatoes

- 1 teaspoon dried thyme

- 1 teaspoon dried rosemary

- 1/2 teaspoon black pepper

- 1/2 teaspoon salt

- 2 cups cooked quinoa

- 1 tablespoon fresh basil, chopped (for garnish)

Instructions:

1. Turn on your oven and set it to 375°F (190°C).

2. In a large mixing bowl, add the eggplant, zucchini, yellow bell pepper, red bell pepper, chopped onion, minced garlic, olive oil, dried thyme, dried rosemary, black pepper, and salt. Toss well to coat the vegetables evenly.

3. Spread the coated vegetables in a single layer on a baking sheet.

4. Roast the vegetables in the preheated oven for 25-30 minutes, or until tender and slightly caramelized.

5. While the vegetables are roasting, prepare the quinoa according to package instructions.

6. In a large skillet, add the roasted vegetables and low-sodium diced tomatoes. Heat over medium heat for 5-7 minutes to meld the flavors.

7. Serve the ratatouille over cooked herbed quinoa.

8. Garnish with fresh basil.

Nutritional Information (per serving):

- Carbs: 49 grams

- Phosphorus: 302 mg

- Potassium: 871 mg

- Sodium: 278 mg
- Protein: 11 grams

Baked Cod with Herbed Quinoa

Prep Time: 15 minutes **Cook Time:** 20 minutes **Servings:** 4

Ingredients:

- 4 cod fillets (about 6 ounces each)
- 2 cups quinoa
- 4 cups low-sodium vegetable broth
- 2 tablespoons fresh parsley, chopped
- 2 tablespoons fresh dill, chopped
- 2 tablespoons fresh chives, chopped
- 1 lemon, zest and juice
- 1/4 teaspoon black pepper
- 1/4 teaspoon salt
- 1/4 teaspoon garlic powder
- 1/4 teaspoon onion powder
- 2 tablespoons olive oil

Instructions:

1. Turn on your oven and set it to 375°F (190°C).
2. In a medium saucepan, bring the low-sodium vegetable broth to a boil.
3. Add the quinoa to the boiling broth, reduce the heat to low, cover, and simmer for 15-20 minutes or until the quinoa is cooked and the liquid is absorbed. Fluff the quinoa with a fork.
4. While the quinoa is cooking, prepare the cod fillets. Season them with black pepper, salt, garlic powder, and onion powder.
5. In a small bowl, add the fresh parsley, fresh dill, fresh chives, lemon zest, and lemon juice. Mix sufficiently.

6. Place the seasoned cod fillets in a baking dish and drizzle them with olive oil.

7. Spread the herbed mixture evenly over the cod fillets.

8. Bake the cod in the preheated oven for 15-20 minutes or until the fish flakes easily with a fork.

9. Serve the Baked Cod with Herbed Quinoa hot, with a side of the cooked quinoa.

Nutritional Information (per serving):

- Carbs: 40 grams

- Phosphorus: 279 mg

- Potassium: 453 mg

- Sodium: 392 mg

- Protein: 32 grams

Chicken and Asparagus Foil Packets

Prep Time: 15 minutes **Cook Time:** 25 minutes **Servings:** 4

Ingredients:

- 4 boneless, skinless chicken breasts (about 6 ounces each)

- 1 pound fresh asparagus spears, trimmed

- 4 cloves garlic, minced

- 4 tablespoons olive oil

- 2 tablespoons fresh lemon juice

- 1 teaspoon dried thyme

- 1 teaspoon dried rosemary

- 1/2 teaspoon black pepper

- 1/2 teaspoon salt

- 1 lemon, thinly sliced (for garnish)

- Fresh parsley, chopped (for garnish)

Instructions:

1. Turn on your oven and set it to 425°F (220°C).

2. Cut four large pieces of aluminum foil, each about 12x18 inches in size.

3. Place a chicken breast in the center of each piece of foil.

4. Divide the trimmed asparagus evenly among the foil packets, arranging them around the chicken breasts.

5. In a small bowl, whisk the minced garlic, olive oil, fresh lemon juice, dried thyme, dried rosemary, black pepper, and salt.

6. Drizzle the herb mixture evenly over each chicken breast and asparagus.

7. Place a lemon slice on top of each chicken breast.

8. Fold the sides of the foil over the chicken and asparagus, then fold up the ends to create sealed packets.

9. Place the foil packets on a baking sheet and bake in the preheated oven for 20-25 minutes, or until the chicken is properly cooked and the asparagus is tender.

10. Carefully open the foil packets, garnish with fresh chopped parsley, and serve.

Nutritional Information (per serving):

- Carbs: 6 grams
- Phosphorus: 253 mg
- Potassium: 478 mg
- Sodium: 410 mg
- Protein: 31 grams

Spaghetti Squash Primavera

Prep Time: 15 minutes **Cook Time:** 40 minutes **Servings:** 4

Ingredients:

- 1 large spaghetti squash

- 2 cups cherry tomatoes, halved
- 1 cup sliced zucchini
- 1 cup sliced yellow bell pepper
- 1 cup sliced red bell pepper
- 1 cup sliced mushrooms
- 1/2 cup diced onion
- 2 cloves garlic, minced
- 2 tablespoons olive oil
- 1/4 cup grated Parmesan cheese (optional)
- 1/4 cup fresh basil, chopped (for garnish)
- 1/4 teaspoon black pepper
- 1/4 teaspoon salt
- 1/4 teaspoon dried oregano
- 1/4 teaspoon dried thyme

Instructions:

1. Turn on your oven and set it to 375°F (190°C).

2. Cut the spaghetti squash in half lengthwise and scoop out the seeds. Place the squash halves, cut side down, on a baking sheet lined with parchment paper. Bake in the preheated oven for 35-40 minutes or until the squash flesh is tender.

3. While the squash is baking, heat the olive oil in a large skillet over medium heat.

4. Add the minced garlic and diced onion to the skillet. Sauté for about 2-3 minutes until the onion becomes translucent.

5. Add the sliced zucchini, yellow bell pepper, red bell pepper, and mushrooms to the skillet. Cook for 5-7 minutes, or until the vegetables are tender-crisp.

6. Stir in the halved cherry tomatoes and cook for an extra 2 minutes.

7. Season the vegetable mixture with black pepper, salt, dried oregano, and dried thyme. Mix sufficiently.

8. When the spaghetti squash is done, use a fork to scrape the flesh into spaghetti-like strands.

9. In a large mixing bowl, add the cooked spaghetti squash and the sautéed vegetable mixture. Toss well to combine.

10. If desired, sprinkle grated Parmesan cheese over the Spaghetti Squash Primavera.

11. Garnish with chopped fresh basil.

Nutritional Information (per serving):

- Carbs: 24 grams
- Phosphorus: 244 mg
- Potassium: 534 mg
- Sodium: 319 mg
- Protein: 5 grams

Vegan Lentil Shepherd's Pie

Prep Time: 20 minutes **Cook Time:** 45 minutes **Servings:** 6

Ingredients: For the Filling:

- 1 cup dry green or brown lentils
- 3 cups vegetable broth
- 1 cup diced carrots
- 1 cup diced celery
- 1 cup diced onion
- 2 cloves garlic, minced
- 1 cup frozen peas
- 1 cup frozen corn
- 2 tablespoons olive oil
- 1 teaspoon dried thyme
- 1 teaspoon dried rosemary
- 1/2 teaspoon black pepper

- 1/2 teaspoon salt
- 2 tablespoons tomato paste
- 2 tablespoons low-sodium soy sauce
- 1 tablespoon cornstarch mixed with two tablespoons water (as a thickener)

For the Mashed Potato Topping:

- 4 cups mashed potatoes (prepared with low-sodium broth and unsweetened almond milk)
- 1/4 cup nutritional yeast (optional, for added flavor)
- Salt and pepper to taste

Instructions:

1. Rinse the dry lentils under cold water and drain.

2. In a medium saucepan, add the lentils and vegetable broth. Bring to a boil, then reduce the heat to low, cover, and simmer for 20-25 minutes or until the lentils are tender but not mushy. Drain any excess liquid.

3. While the lentils are cooking, prepare the mashed potatoes using low-sodium vegetable broth and unsweetened almond milk. Mash until smooth and season with nutritional yeast (if using), salt, and pepper. Set aside.

4. Turn on your oven and set it to 375°F (190°C).

5. In a large skillet, heat the olive oil over medium heat. Add the diced carrots, celery, and onion. Sauté for about 5 minutes until the vegetables begin to soften.

6. Add the minced garlic, dried thyme, dried rosemary, black pepper, and salt to the skillet. Sauté for an extra 2 minutes until the garlic is fragrant.

7. Stir in the tomato paste and low-sodium soy sauce. Cook for an extra 2 minutes.

8. Add the cooked lentils, frozen peas, frozen corn, and the cornstarch-water mixture to the skillet. Mix sufficiently and cook for 5-7 minutes until the mixture thickens.

9. Transfer the lentil and vegetable filling to a baking dish.

10. Spread the mashed potato topping evenly over the filling.

11. Place the baking dish in the preheated oven and bake for 20-25 minutes, or until the top is golden brown and the filling is bubbling.

12. Serve the Vegan Lentil Shepherd's Pie hot.

Nutritional Information (per serving):

- Carbs: 55 grams
- Phosphorus: 281 mg
- Potassium: 769 mg
- Sodium: 470 mg
- Protein: 12 grams

Lemon Dill Baked Tilapia

Prep Time: 10 minutes **Cook Time:** 20 minutes **Servings:** 4

Ingredients:

- 4 tilapia fillets (about 6 ounces each)
- 2 tablespoons olive oil
- 2 tablespoons fresh lemon juice
- 1 tablespoon fresh dill, chopped
- 2 cloves garlic, minced
- 1/2 teaspoon black pepper
- 1/2 teaspoon salt
- 1 lemon, thinly sliced (for garnish)

Instructions:

1. Turn on your oven and set it to 375°F (190°C).

2. In a small bowl, whisk the olive oil, fresh lemon juice, chopped fresh dill, minced garlic, black pepper, and salt.

3. Place the tilapia fillets in a baking dish large enough to accommodate them in a single layer.

4. Pour the lemon dill mixture evenly over the tilapia fillets.

5. Lay lemon slices on top of the tilapia for garnish.

6. Cover the baking dish with aluminum foil.

7. Bake in the preheated oven for 15-20 minutes, or until the tilapia flakes easily with a fork and is properly cooked.

8. Serve the Lemon Dill Baked Tilapia hot, garnished with additional fresh dill if desired.

Nutritional Information (per serving):

- Carbs: 1 gram

- Phosphorus: 215 mg

- Potassium: 360 mg

- Sodium: 356 mg

- Protein: 30 grams

Stuffed Portobello Mushrooms with Spinach and Feta

Prep Time: 20 minutes **Cook Time:** 25 minutes **Servings:** 4

Ingredients:

- 4 large portobello mushrooms

- 2 cups fresh spinach, chopped

- 1/2 cup crumbled feta cheese (low-sodium, if available)

- 1/4 cup chopped red bell pepper

- 1/4 cup chopped red onion

- 2 cloves garlic, minced

- 2 tablespoons olive oil

- 1/2 teaspoon dried oregano

- 1/2 teaspoon dried basil

- 1/4 teaspoon black pepper

- 1/4 teaspoon salt

Instructions:

1. Turn on your oven and set it to 375°F (190°C).

2. Take out the stems from the portobello mushrooms and gently scrape out the gills using a spoon. Place the mushrooms on a baking sheet lined with parchment paper.

3. In a large skillet, heat the olive oil over medium heat.

4. Add the minced garlic, chopped red onion, and chopped red bell pepper to the skillet. Sauté for 2-3 minutes until the vegetables begin to soften.

5. Stir in the chopped spinach and keep on cooking for an extra 2-3 minutes until the spinach wilts.

6. Take out the skillet from heat and stir in the crumbled feta cheese, dried oregano, dried basil, black pepper, and salt. Mix sufficiently to combine.

7. Divide the spinach and feta mixture evenly among the hollowed-out portobello mushrooms, packing it down slightly.

8. Place the stuffed mushrooms in the preheated oven and bake for 20-25 minutes, or until the mushrooms are tender and the filling is heated through.

9. Serve the Stuffed Portobello Mushrooms with Spinach and Feta hot.

Nutritional Information (per serving):

- Carbs: 10 grams
- Phosphorus: 187 mg
- Potassium: 602 mg
- Sodium: 374 mg
- Protein: 6 grams

SNACKS

Almond and Berry Protein Bites

Prep Time: 15 minutes
Cook Time: 0 minutes
Number of Servings: 12 bites

Ingredients:

- 1 cup unsalted almonds, finely chopped
- 1/2 cup dried berries (such as cranberries or blueberries), finely chopped
- 1/2 cup vanilla protein powder
- 1/4 cup almond butter
- 1/4 cup honey
- 1/2 teaspoon vanilla extract
- 1/4 teaspoon salt
- 2 tablespoons ground flaxseed

Instructions:

1. In a large mixing bowl, add the finely chopped unsalted almonds, dried berries, and vanilla protein powder.

2. In a microwave-safe bowl, warm the almond butter and honey together for about 30 seconds, or until they become smooth and well-mixed.

3. Stir in the vanilla extract, salt, and ground flaxseed into the almond butter and honey mixture.

4. Pour the almond butter mixture over the dry ingredients in the large mixing bowl.

5. Mix all the ingredients together until well combined. The mixture should be sticky and hold together when pressed.

6. Using clean hands, take approximately one tablespoon of the mixture at a time and roll it into a bite-sized ball. Repeat this process until you have formed 12 protein bites.

7. Place the protein bites on a baking sheet lined with parchment paper.

8. Refrigerate the bites for at least 30 minutes to help them firm up.

9. Once chilled, the Almond and Berry Protein Bites are ready to serve. Enjoy!

Nutritional Information (per serving):

- Carbs: 15 grams

- Phosphorus: 80 milligrams

- Potassium: 120 milligrams

- Sodium: 40 milligrams

- Protein: 8 grams

Roasted Edamame with Sea Salt

Prep Time: 5 minutes
Cook Time: 15 minutes
Number of Servings: 4 servings

Ingredients:

- 2 cups frozen edamame (unshelled)

- 1 tablespoon olive oil

- 1/2 teaspoon sea salt

Instructions:

1. Turn on your oven and set it to 425°F (220°C).

2. In a large mixing bowl, add the frozen edamame, olive oil, and sea salt.

3. Toss the edamame in the bowl until evenly coated with the olive oil and sea salt.

4. Spread the seasoned edamame in a single layer on a baking sheet lined with parchment paper.

5. Place the baking sheet in the preheated oven and roast the edamame for 15 minutes, or until they become lightly golden and crispy.

6. Take out the roasted edamame from the oven and let them cool slightly before serving.

7. Serve the Roasted Edamame with Sea Salt as a nutritious snack or appetizer.

Nutritional Information (per serving):

- Carbs: 9 grams

- Phosphorus: 90 milligrams

- Potassium: 160 milligrams

- Sodium: 295 milligrams

- Protein: 8 grams

Celery and Peanut Butter

Prep Time: 5 minutes
Cook Time: 0 minutes
Number of Servings: 2 servings

Ingredients:

- 4 stalks of celery, cleaned and trimmed

- 4 tablespoons unsalted peanut butter

Instructions:

1. Take the cleaned and trimmed celery stalks and cut them into 4-inch pieces.

2. In a small bowl, measure out 4 tablespoons of unsalted peanut butter.

3. Using a butter knife, spread the peanut butter evenly into the celery stalks' hollow centers.

4. Arrange the Celery and Peanut Butter sticks on a serving platter.

5. Your Celery and Peanut Butter snack is now ready to be enjoyed!

Nutritional Information (per serving):

- Carbs: 5 grams

- Phosphorus: 50 milligrams

- Potassium: 200 milligrams
- Sodium: 70 milligrams
- Protein: 4 grams

Cottage Cheese with Pineapple

Prep Time: 5 minutes
Cook Time: 0 minutes
Number of Servings: 2 servings

Ingredients:

- 1 cup low-fat cottage cheese
- 1 cup fresh pineapple chunks

Instructions:

1. In a bowl, measure out one cup of low-fat cottage cheese.
2. Next, measure out one cup of fresh pineapple chunks.
3. Combine the cottage cheese and pineapple chunks in a serving bowl.
4. Gently stir the mixture until the pineapple is evenly distributed throughout the cottage cheese.
5. Your Cottage Cheese with Pineapple is now ready to serve. Enjoy!

Nutritional Information (per serving):

- Carbs: 15 grams
- Phosphorus: 180 milligrams
- Potassium: 180 milligrams
- Sodium: 380 milligrams
- Protein: 13 grams

Carrot and Cucumber Sticks with Hummus

Prep Time: 10 minutes
Cook Time: 0 minutes
Number of Servings: 2 servings

Ingredients:

- 2 medium carrots, peeled and cut into sticks
- 1 medium cucumber, cut into sticks
- 1/2 cup low-sodium hummus

Instructions:

1. Begin by preparing the carrot sticks. Peel two medium carrots and cut them into sticks. Measure out and prepare approximately two cups of carrot sticks.

2. Next, take one medium cucumber and cut it into sticks as well. Measure out and prepare approximately two cups of cucumber sticks.

3. In a small bowl, measure out 1/2 cup of low-sodium hummus.

4. Arrange the carrot and cucumber sticks on a serving platter.

5. Serve the Carrot and Cucumber Sticks with the prepared hummus for dipping.

6. Enjoy your nutritious snack!

Nutritional Information (per serving):

- Carbs: 20 grams
- Phosphorus: 90 milligrams
- Potassium: 400 milligrams
- Sodium: 150 milligrams
- Protein: 6 grams

Greek Yogurt with Honey and Walnuts

Prep Time: 5 minutes
Cook Time: 0 minutes
Number of Servings: 2 servings

Ingredients:

- 2 cups plain Greek yogurt
- 2 tablespoons honey

- 1/4 cup chopped walnuts

Instructions:

1. Begin by measuring out two cups of plain Greek yogurt.

2. In a small bowl, measure out two tablespoons of honey.

3. Chop 1/4 cup of walnuts and set them aside.

4. In individual serving bowls or glasses, divide the two cups of Greek yogurt equally.

5. Drizzle one tablespoon of honey over each portion of Greek yogurt.

6. Sprinkle two tablespoons of chopped walnuts evenly over the yogurt and honey in each serving.

7. Your Greek Yogurt with Honey and Walnuts is now ready to enjoy as a delicious and balanced snack or dessert.

Nutritional Information (per serving):

- Carbs: 16 grams
- Phosphorus: 130 milligrams
- Potassium: 200 milligrams
- Sodium: 50 milligrams
- Protein: 14 grams

Baked Sweet Potato Fries
Prep Time: 15 minutes
Cook Time: 25 minutes
Number of Servings: 4 servings

Ingredients:

- 4 medium sweet potatoes
- 2 tablespoons olive oil
- 1/2 teaspoon salt
- 1/4 teaspoon black pepper
- 1/4 teaspoon paprika (optional)

Instructions:

1. Turn on your oven and set it to 425°F (220°C).

2. Wash and peel the 4 medium sweet potatoes. Cut them into fries of approximately 1/2-inch width.

3. In a large bowl, drizzle two tablespoons of olive oil over the sweet potato fries. Toss to ensure that all the fries are evenly coated with the oil.

4. Season the fries with 1/2 teaspoon of salt, 1/4 teaspoon of black pepper, and 1/4 teaspoon of paprika (optional).

5. Arrange the seasoned sweet potato fries in a single layer on a baking sheet.

6. Place the baking sheet in the preheated oven and bake for about 25 minutes, turning the fries halfway through, until golden and crispy.

7. Once the Baked Sweet Potato Fries are cooked to your desired crispiness, remove them from the oven.

8. Serve the fries immediately as a tasty and nutritious side dish or snack.

Nutritional Information (per serving):

- Carbs: 30 grams

- Phosphorus: 90 milligrams

- Potassium: 550 milligrams

- Sodium: 325 milligrams

- Protein: 2 grams

Baked Sweet Potato Fries
Prep Time: 15 minutes
Cook Time: 30 minutes
Number of Servings: 4

Ingredients:

- 4 medium sweet potatoes, peeled and cut into 1/4-inch thick strips

- 2 tablespoons olive oil

- 1/2 teaspoon salt
- 1/4 teaspoon black pepper
- 1/4 teaspoon garlic powder
- 1/4 teaspoon paprika
- 1/4 teaspoon onion powder
- Cooking spray

Instructions:

1. Turn on your oven and set it to 425°F (220°C) and line a baking sheet with parchment paper.

2. In a large bowl, add the sweet potato strips, olive oil, salt, black pepper, garlic powder, paprika, and onion powder. Toss until the sweet potato strips are evenly coated with the seasonings and oil.

3. Spread the seasoned sweet potato strips in a single layer on the prepared baking sheet. Ensure not crowded to allow even cooking.

4. Lightly spray the sweet potato strips with cooking spray. This will help them become crispy during baking.

5. Place the baking sheet in the preheated oven and bake for 25-30 minutes, or until the sweet potato fries are golden brown and crisp. Make sure to flip the fries halfway through the cooking time to ensure even browning.

6. Once done, take out the sweet potato fries from the oven and let them cool slightly before serving.

Nutritional Information (Per Serving):

- Carbohydrates: 30g
- Phosphorus: 125mg
- Potassium: 490mg
- Sodium: 320mg
- Protein: 2g

Avocado Slices with Lime and Chili

Prep Time: 10 minutes
Cook Time: 0 minutes
Number of Servings: 4

Ingredients:

- 2 ripe avocados, peeled, pitted, and sliced
- 2 limes, juiced
- 1/4 teaspoon chili powder
- 1/4 teaspoon salt
- 1/8 teaspoon black pepper
- 1/8 teaspoon garlic powder

Instructions:

1. Start by slicing the ripe avocados and arranging them neatly on a serving platter.

2. In a small bowl, add the lime juice, chili powder, salt, black pepper, and garlic powder. Mix sufficiently to create a flavorful dressing.

3. Drizzle the lime and chili dressing evenly over the avocado slices. Ensure that each slice gets a generous coating of the dressing.

4. Allow the flavors to meld for a few minutes before serving. You can let the dish sit for about 5 minutes to let the avocados absorb the zesty dressing.

5. Serve your avocado slices with lime and chili as a refreshing and zesty side dish or appetizer.

Nutritional Information (Per Serving):

- Carbohydrates: 9g
- Phosphorus: 75mg
- Potassium: 380mg
- Sodium: 160mg
- Protein: 2g

Popcorn Seasoned with Herbs and Nutritional Yeast

Prep Time: 5 minutes
Cook Time: 5 minutes
Number of Servings: 4

Ingredients:

- 1/2 cup popcorn kernels

- 2 tablespoons olive oil

- 2 tablespoons nutritional yeast

- 1/2 teaspoon dried basil

- 1/2 teaspoon dried oregano

- 1/2 teaspoon garlic powder

- 1/4 teaspoon salt

- 1/4 teaspoon black pepper

Instructions:

1. Heat the olive oil in a large pot with a lid over medium heat. Add three popcorn kernels to the pot and cover it with the lid.

2. Wait for the test kernels to pop. Once they do, remove them from the pot.

3. Add the remaining popcorn kernels to the pot, ensuring they form an even layer.

4. Cover the pot with the lid and shake it occasionally to prevent burning. Continue to heat until the popping slows down to about 2 seconds between pops. This should take approximately 3-5 minutes.

5. While the popcorn is popping, in a small bowl, add the nutritional yeast, dried basil, dried oregano, garlic powder, salt, and black pepper. Mix sufficiently to create the seasoning blend.

6. Once the popcorn is done, take out the pot from the heat. Carefully open the lid away from your face to avoid steam.

7. While the popcorn is still hot, drizzle the olive oil over the popcorn and toss it gently to ensure even distribution.

8. Sprinkle the prepared seasoning blend over the popcorn, again tossing to coat the popcorn evenly with the herbs and nutritional yeast.

9. Allow the popcorn to cool slightly before serving.

Nutritional Information (Per Serving):

- Carbohydrates: 21g
- Phosphorus: 75mg
- Potassium: 90mg
- Sodium: 150mg
- Protein: 3g

Pickle Spears Wrapped in Deli Turkey

Prep Time: 10 minutes
Cook Time: 0 minutes
Number of Servings: 4

Ingredients:

- 8 dill pickle spears
- 8 slices deli turkey
- 1/4 cup cream cheese (low-fat, if desired)
- 1/4 teaspoon garlic powder
- 1/4 teaspoon black pepper
- 1/4 teaspoon dried dill weed

Instructions:

1. In a small bowl, add the cream cheese, garlic powder, black pepper, and dried dill weed. Mix sufficiently to create a flavorful cream cheese spread.

2. Lay out a slice of deli turkey on a clean surface.

3. Spread approximately 1/2 tablespoon of the cream cheese mixture evenly over the turkey slice.

4. Place a dill pickle spear at one end of the turkey slice and roll it up tightly, ensuring the pickle is securely wrapped within the turkey slice.

5. Repeat steps 2-4 for the remaining pickle spears and turkey slices.

6. Once all pickle spears are wrapped, you can serve them immediately or refrigerate until ready to serve.

7. Optionally, you can slice each pickle spear wrap into bite-sized pieces for easier handling.

Nutritional Information (Per Serving):

- Carbohydrates: 2g

- Phosphorus: 65mg

- Potassium: 110mg

- Sodium: 580mg

- Protein: 6g

Cucumber and Greek Yogurt Dip

Prep Time: 10 minutes
Cook Time: 0 minutes
Number of Servings: 4

Ingredients:

- 1 cup low-fat Greek yogurt

- 1 cucumber, finely grated and drained

- 1 clove garlic, minced

- 1 tablespoon fresh dill, finely chopped

- 1/4 teaspoon salt

- 1/4 teaspoon black pepper

- 1/4 teaspoon lemon juice

Instructions:

1. Begin by grating the cucumber using a fine grater. Place the grated cucumber in a clean kitchen towel or cheesecloth and squeeze out any excess liquid. You should be left with about 1/2 cup of drained cucumber.

2. In a mixing bowl, add the low-fat Greek yogurt and the drained, grated cucumber.

3. Add the minced garlic, finely chopped fresh dill, salt, black pepper, and lemon juice to the bowl with the yogurt and cucumber. Mix everything together until well combined.

4. Taste the dip and adjust the seasoning if necessary, adding more salt, pepper, or lemon juice to suit your preference.

5. Refrigerate the cucumber and Greek yogurt dip for at least 30 minutes before serving. Chilling will allow the flavors to meld.

6. Serve the dip with fresh vegetable sticks or whole-grain crackers.

Nutritional Information (Per Serving):

- Carbohydrates: 6g

- Phosphorus: 80mg

- Potassium: 230mg

- Sodium: 240mg

- Protein: 6g

Roasted Red Pepper and Walnut Hummus

Prep Time: 15 minutes
Cook Time: 0 minutes
Number of Servings: 6

Ingredients:

- 1 can (15 ounces) chickpeas, drained and rinsed

- 1/2 cup roasted red peppers, chopped

- 1/4 cup walnuts

- 2 cloves garlic, minced

- 2 tablespoons lemon juice

- 2 tablespoons olive oil

- 1/2 teaspoon cumin

- 1/4 teaspoon salt

- 1/4 teaspoon black pepper

- 2 tablespoons fresh parsley, chopped (for garnish, optional)

Instructions:

1. In a food processor, add the drained and rinsed chickpeas, chopped roasted red peppers, walnuts, minced garlic, lemon juice, olive oil, cumin, salt, and black pepper.

2. Process the mixture until it becomes smooth and creamy, scraping down the sides of the bowl as needed. If the hummus seems too thick, you can add a tablespoon of water at a time to reach your desired consistency.

3. Taste the hummus and adjust the seasoning if needed by adding more salt, pepper, or lemon juice.

4. Transfer the roasted red pepper and walnut hummus to a serving bowl.

5. If desired, garnish with chopped fresh parsley.

6. Serve the hummus with vegetable sticks, whole-grain pita bread, or your choice of dippers.

Nutritional Information (Per Serving):

- Carbohydrates: 15g

- Phosphorus: 90mg

- Potassium: 180mg

- Sodium: 220mg

- Protein: 5g

Cherry Tomato and Mozzarella Skewers

Prep Time: 15 minutes
Cook Time: 0 minutes
Number of Servings: 4

Ingredients:

- 1 pint cherry tomatoes
- 8 small fresh mozzarella balls (bocconcini)
- 8 fresh basil leaves
- 2 tablespoons balsamic vinegar
- 1 tablespoon olive oil
- 1/4 teaspoon salt
- 1/4 teaspoon black pepper
- 8 wooden skewers (6 inches), soaked in water

Instructions:

1. Begin by assembling the skewers. On each wooden skewer, thread a cherry tomato, a fresh mozzarella ball, and a fresh basil leaf. Repeat this process until all the skewers are assembled.
2. In a small bowl, whisk the balsamic vinegar, olive oil, salt, and black pepper to create a simple vinaigrette.
3. Drizzle the vinaigrette evenly over the cherry tomato and mozzarella skewers.
4. Place the skewers on a serving platter or dish.
5. Optionally, you can serve any remaining vinaigrette on the side for dipping.
6. Serve the cherry tomato and mozzarella skewers immediately as a delicious appetizer or side dish.

Nutritional Information (Per Serving):

- Carbohydrates: 5g
- Phosphorus: 70mg
- Potassium: 260mg
- Sodium: 190mg
- Protein: 7g

Almond and Coconut Energy Balls
Prep Time: 15 minutes
Cook Time: 0 minutes
Number of Servings: 12

Ingredients:

- 1 cup almonds
- 1/2 cup unsweetened shredded coconut
- 1/4 cup almond butter (no added salt)
- 1/4 cup honey (or a sugar substitute suitable for diabetics)
- 1/2 teaspoon vanilla extract
- 1/4 teaspoon salt

Instructions:

1. In a food processor, add the almonds and pulse until finely chopped, but not too fine. You want some texture in the energy balls.
2. Transfer the chopped almonds to a mixing bowl.
3. To the bowl with almonds, add the unsweetened shredded coconut, almond butter, honey (or sugar substitute), vanilla extract, and salt.
4. Mix all the ingredients together until well combined.
5. With clean hands, take approximately one tablespoon of the mixture and roll it into a ball. Repeat this process until all the mixture is used up, making approximately 12 energy balls.
6. Place the energy balls on a plate or tray lined with parchment paper.
7. Refrigerate the energy balls for at least 30 minutes to help them firm up.
8. Once chilled, the energy balls are ready to serve. Store any leftovers in an airtight container in the refrigerator.

Nutritional Information (Per Serving):

- Carbohydrates: 10g
- Phosphorus: 85mg

- Potassium: 120mg

- Sodium: 45mg

- Protein: 4g

Cottage Cheese with Sliced Peaches

Prep Time: 5 minutes
Cook Time: 0 minutes
Number of Servings: 2

Ingredients:

- 1 cup low-fat cottage cheese

- 2 ripe peaches, sliced

- 1/4 teaspoon cinnamon (optional)

- 1/4 teaspoon vanilla extract (optional)

- 1 tablespoon honey (or a sugar substitute suitable for diabetics)

Instructions:

1. In a mixing bowl, add the low-fat cottage cheese, sliced peaches, and optional cinnamon and vanilla extract if desired.

2. Gently stir the mixture to evenly distribute the peaches throughout the cottage cheese.

3. Drizzle the honey (or sugar substitute) over the top of the cottage cheese and peaches.

4. Stir again, gently incorporating the honey into the mixture.

5. Divide the cottage cheese and peach mixture into two serving bowls.

6. Optionally, you can garnish with a sprinkle of additional cinnamon or a few slices of fresh peach.

7. Serve immediately and enjoy as a delicious and nutritious snack or breakfast.

Nutritional Information (Per Serving):

- Carbohydrates: 23g

- Phosphorus: 260mg

- Potassium: 410mg

- Sodium: 440mg

- Protein: 14g

Roasted Brussels Sprouts Chips
Prep Time: 10 minutes
Cook Time: 20 minutes
Number of Servings: 4

Ingredients:

- 1 pound Brussels sprouts, trimmed and halved

- 2 tablespoons olive oil

- 1/4 teaspoon salt

- 1/4 teaspoon black pepper

- 1/4 teaspoon garlic powder

- 1/4 teaspoon onion powder

- Cooking spray

Instructions:

1. Turn on your oven and set it to 375°F (190°C) and line a baking sheet with parchment paper.

2. In a large bowl, add the halved Brussels sprouts, olive oil, salt, black pepper, garlic powder, and onion powder. Toss until the Brussels sprouts are evenly coated with the seasonings and oil.

3. Spread the seasoned Brussels sprouts in a single layer on the prepared baking sheet. Make sure not crowded to allow even cooking.

4. Lightly spray the Brussels sprouts with cooking spray. This will help them become crispy during roasting.

5. Place the baking sheet in the preheated oven and roast for 15-20 minutes, or until the Brussels sprouts chips are golden brown and

crisp. Be sure to flip them halfway through the cooking time for even browning.

6. Once done, take out the Brussels sprouts chips from the oven and let them cool slightly before serving.

Nutritional Information (Per Serving):

- Carbohydrates: 9g

- Phosphorus: 75mg

- Potassium: 350mg

- Sodium: 150mg

- Protein: 3g

Carrot and Zucchini Fritters

Prep Time: 15 minutes
Cook Time: 15 minutes
Number of Servings: 4

Ingredients:

- 2 cups grated carrots

- 2 cups grated zucchini

- 1/4 cup finely chopped onion

- 2 large eggs

- 1/4 cup whole wheat flour

- 1/4 cup grated Parmesan cheese

- 1/2 teaspoon garlic powder

- 1/2 teaspoon onion powder

- 1/4 teaspoon salt

- 1/4 teaspoon black pepper

- Cooking spray

Instructions:

1. Begin by grating the carrots and zucchini. Place them in a clean kitchen towel or cheesecloth and squeeze out any excess moisture.

2. In a mixing bowl, add the grated carrots, grated zucchini, finely chopped onion, eggs, whole wheat flour, grated Parmesan cheese, garlic powder, onion powder, salt, and black pepper.

3. Mix all the ingredients together until well combined.

4. Heat a non-stick skillet over medium heat and lightly coat it with cooking spray.

5. Spoon approximately 1/4 cup of the carrot and zucchini mixture onto the skillet for each fritter, pressing it down gently to flatten.

6. Cook the fritters for about 3-4 minutes on each side, or until golden brown and properly cooked.

7. Take out the fritters from the skillet and place them on a plate lined with paper towels to absorb any excess oil.

8. Repeat the process with the remaining mixture, adding more cooking spray to the skillet as needed.

9. Serve the carrot and zucchini fritters hot as a delicious and nutritious side dish.

Nutritional Information (Per Serving):

- Carbohydrates: 14g
- Phosphorus: 150mg
- Potassium: 390mg
- Sodium: 300mg
- Protein: 7g

DESSERTS

Sugar-Free Mixed Berry Sorbet

Prep Time: 10 minutes
Cook Time: 0 minutes
Number of Servings: 4

Ingredients:

- 2 cups mixed berries (strawberries, blueberries, raspberries)
- 1/4 cup erythritol (sugar substitute)
- 1/4 cup water
- 1 teaspoon lemon juice
- 1/2 teaspoon vanilla extract

Instructions:

1. Wash the mixed berries thoroughly and remove any stems or leaves.

2. In a small saucepan, add the erythritol and water. Heat over low heat, stirring constantly, until the erythritol is completely dissolved. This should take about 2-3 minutes. Take it out from heat and let it cool.

3. Place the mixed berries, erythritol syrup, lemon juice, and vanilla extract in a blender or food processor.

4. Blend the mixture until it becomes smooth and well combined.

5. Pour the berry mixture into a shallow, freezer-safe container.

6. Cover the container and place it in the freezer for about 4 hours or until the sorbet is firm, stirring every hour to break up any ice crystals.

7. Once the sorbet has set, scoop it into serving bowls or glasses.

8. Garnish with fresh berries if desired, and serve immediately.

Nutritional Information (Per Serving):

- Carbs: 14g

- Phosphorus: 30mg

- Potassium: 120mg

- Sodium: 5mg

- Protein: 1g

Chocolate Avocado Mousse

Prep Time: 10 minutes
Cook Time: 0 minutes
Number of Servings: 4

Ingredients:

- 2 ripe avocados

- 1/4 cup unsweetened cocoa powder

- 1/4 cup erythritol (sugar substitute)

- 1/4 cup almond milk

- 1 teaspoon vanilla extract

- 1/4 teaspoon salt

Instructions:

1. Cut the avocados in half, take out the pits, and scoop the flesh into a blender or food processor.

2. Add the unsweetened cocoa powder, erythritol, almond milk, vanilla extract, and salt to the blender with the avocados.

3. Blend the mixture until it becomes smooth and creamy. You may need to stop and scrape down the sides of the blender to ensure everything is well combined.

4. Taste the mousse and adjust the sweetness to your liking by adding more erythritol if needed.

5. Once the mousse is smooth and sweetened to your preference, spoon it into serving bowls or glasses.

6. Refrigerate for at least 30 minutes to allow the mousse to chill and set.

7. Serve chilled, garnished with a sprinkle of cocoa powder or grated dark chocolate if desired.

Nutritional Information (Per Serving):

- Carbs: 10g

- Phosphorus: 70mg

- Potassium: 400mg

- Sodium: 75mg

- Protein: 3g

Baked Apples with Cinnamon and Walnuts

Prep Time: 15 minutes
Cook Time: 30 minutes
Number of Servings: 4

Ingredients:

- 4 large apples (such as Granny Smith or Fuji)

- 2 tablespoons chopped walnuts

- 1 tablespoon erythritol (sugar substitute)

- 1 teaspoon ground cinnamon

- 1/4 teaspoon salt

- 1/4 cup water

- 1 teaspoon lemon juice

- 1/2 teaspoon vanilla extract

Instructions:

1. Turn on your oven and set it to 375°F (190°C).

2. Wash the apples and then carefully core them, removing the seeds and creating a small well in the center of each apple, leaving the bottom intact.

3. In a small bowl, add the chopped walnuts, erythritol, ground cinnamon, and salt. Mix these ingredients together.

4. Stuff each apple with an equal amount of the walnut mixture, filling the wells you created in step 2.

5. Place the stuffed apples in a baking dish.

6. In a separate bowl, mix together the water, lemon juice, and vanilla extract.

7. Pour this mixture over the apples in the baking dish.

8. Cover the dish with aluminum foil.

9. Bake the apples in the preheated oven for 30 minutes or until tender. You can check their doneness by inserting a fork; it should go through easily.

10. Once baked, take out the foil and let the apples cool slightly before serving.

Nutritional Information (Per Serving):

- Carbs: 20g

- Phosphorus: 75mg

- Potassium: 250mg

- Sodium: 70mg

- Protein: 1g

Greek Yogurt Popsicles with Mango

Prep Time: 15 minutes
Cook Time: 0 minutes
Number of Servings: 6

Ingredients:

- 1 1/2 cups plain Greek yogurt

- 1 1/2 cups diced ripe mango (about 2 small mangoes)

- 2 tablespoons erythritol (sugar substitute)

- 1 teaspoon vanilla extract

Instructions:

1. In a blender or food processor, add the plain Greek yogurt, diced ripe mango, erythritol, and vanilla extract.

2. Blend the mixture until it's smooth and well combined.

3. Taste the mixture and adjust the sweetness to your liking by adding more erythritol if needed.

4. Pour the mango and yogurt mixture into popsicle molds.

5. Insert popsicle sticks into the center of each mold.

6. Place the molds in the freezer and let them freeze for at least 4-6 hours or until completely solid.

7. To take out the popsicles from the molds, run warm water over the outside of the molds for a few seconds to loosen them.

8. Serve the Greek yogurt popsicles with mango immediately or store them in an airtight container in the freezer for later.

Nutritional Information (Per Serving):

- Carbs: 15g
- Phosphorus: 125mg
- Potassium: 210mg
- Sodium: 40mg
- Protein: 6g

Chia Seed Pudding with Berries
Prep Time: 10 minutes
Cook Time: 0 minutes
Number of Servings: 4

Ingredients:

- 1/2 cup chia seeds
- 2 cups unsweetened almond milk
- 1/4 cup erythritol (sugar substitute)
- 1 teaspoon vanilla extract
- 1 cup mixed berries (strawberries, blueberries, raspberries)

Instructions:

1. In a mixing bowl, add the chia seeds, unsweetened almond milk, erythritol, and vanilla extract.

2. Stir the mixture well to ensure the chia seeds are evenly distributed.

3. Let the mixture sit for 5 minutes, then stir again to prevent clumping.

4. Cover the bowl with plastic wrap or a lid and refrigerate for at least 4 hours or overnight. This allows the chia seeds to absorb the liquid and create a pudding-like consistency.

5. Before serving, stir the chia seed pudding to make sure it's smooth and not lumpy.

6. Divide the pudding into serving bowls or glasses.

7. Top each serving with a generous portion of mixed berries.

8. Serve the chia seed pudding with berries chilled and enjoy!

Nutritional Information (Per Serving):

- Carbs: 15g

- Phosphorus: 120mg

- Potassium: 160mg

- Sodium: 70mg

- Protein: 5g

Almond Flour Brownies
Prep Time: 15 minutes
Cook Time: 25 minutes
Number of Servings: 9

Ingredients:

- 1 1/2 cups almond flour

- 1/2 cup unsweetened cocoa powder

- 1/2 cup erythritol (sugar substitute)

- 1/2 teaspoon baking powder

- 1/4 teaspoon salt
- 1/2 cup unsalted butter
- 2 large eggs
- 1 teaspoon vanilla extract
- 1/4 cup unsweetened almond milk

Instructions:

1. Turn on your oven and set it to 350°F (175°C). Grease an 8x8-inch baking pan and line it with parchment paper for easy removal.

2. In a mixing bowl, add the almond flour, unsweetened cocoa powder, erythritol, baking powder, and salt. Mix these dry ingredients together.

3. In a separate microwave-safe bowl, melt the unsalted butter in the microwave or on the stovetop until it's completely liquid.

4. Add the melted butter to the dry ingredient mixture and stir until well combined.

5. In a small bowl, whisk the eggs, vanilla extract, and unsweetened almond milk together.

6. Pour the egg mixture into the dry ingredient and butter mixture, and stir until you have a smooth batter.

7. Pour the brownie batter into the prepared baking pan and spread it out evenly.

8. Bake in the preheated oven for approximately 25 minutes or until a toothpick inserted into the center comes out with just a few moist crumbs.

9. Take out the brownies from the oven and let them cool in the pan for about 10 minutes.

10. Lift the brownies out of the pan using the parchment paper and place them on a wire rack to cool completely.

11. Once cooled, cut the brownies into 9 squares.

Nutritional Information (Per Serving):

- Carbs: 6g

- Phosphorus: 50mg

- Potassium: 20mg

- Sodium: 95mg

- Protein: 4g

Coconut and Lime Energy Bites
Prep Time: 15 minutes
Cook Time: 0 minutes
Number of Servings: 12

Ingredients:

- 1 cup unsweetened shredded coconut

- 1/2 cup almond flour

- 1/4 cup erythritol (sugar substitute)

- Zest of 1 lime

- 2 tablespoons lime juice

- 2 tablespoons coconut oil, melted

- 1/2 teaspoon vanilla extract

- 1/4 teaspoon salt

Instructions:

1. In a mixing bowl, add the unsweetened shredded coconut, almond flour, erythritol, lime zest, and salt.

2. In a separate small bowl, whisk the lime juice, melted coconut oil, and vanilla extract.

3. Pour the wet mixture over the dry ingredients in the mixing bowl.

4. Stir until all the ingredients are well combined and the mixture becomes sticky.

5. Using clean hands, take about one tablespoon of the mixture and roll it into a ball. Repeat this step to form 12 energy bites.

6. Place the energy bites on a plate or tray lined with parchment paper.

7. Refrigerate the energy bites for at least 30 minutes to firm them up.

8. Once chilled, transfer the energy bites to an airtight container for storage.

Nutritional Information (Per Serving):

- Carbs: 4g
- Phosphorus: 25mg
- Potassium: 30mg
- Sodium: 35mg
- Protein: 1g

Pumpkin Pie Smoothie

Prep Time: 5 minutes
Cook Time: 0 minutes
Number of Servings: 2

Ingredients:

- 1 cup canned pumpkin puree
- 1 1/2 cups unsweetened almond milk
- 1/4 cup erythritol (sugar substitute)
- 1 teaspoon ground cinnamon
- 1/2 teaspoon ground nutmeg
- 1/4 teaspoon ground cloves
- 1/4 teaspoon ground ginger
- 1/2 teaspoon vanilla extract
- 1/4 cup plain Greek yogurt

Instructions:

1. In a blender, add the canned pumpkin puree, unsweetened almond milk, erythritol, ground cinnamon, ground nutmeg, ground cloves, ground ginger, and vanilla extract.

2. Blend the mixture until it's smooth and all the ingredients are well incorporated.

3. Taste the smoothie and adjust the sweetness to your liking by adding more erythritol if needed.

4. Add the plain Greek yogurt to the blender and blend again until the smoothie is creamy.

5. Pour the pumpkin pie smoothie into two glasses.

6. If desired, garnish with a sprinkle of ground cinnamon on top.

7. Serve the smoothie immediately and enjoy!

Nutritional Information (Per Serving):

- Carbs: 10g
- Phosphorus: 50mg
- Potassium: 200mg
- Sodium: 100mg
- Protein: 3g

Avocado and Cocoa Smoothie

Prep Time: 5 minutes
Cook Time: 0 minutes
Number of Servings: 2

Ingredients:

- 1 ripe avocado
- 2 tablespoons unsweetened cocoa powder
- 1/4 cup erythritol (sugar substitute)
- 1 1/2 cups unsweetened almond milk
- 1/2 teaspoon vanilla extract
- 1/4 teaspoon salt
- 1/2 cup ice cubes (optional)

Instructions:

1. Cut the ripe avocado in half, take out the pit, and scoop the flesh into a blender.

2. Add the unsweetened cocoa powder, erythritol, unsweetened almond milk, vanilla extract, and salt to the blender with the avocado.

3. If you prefer a colder smoothie, add the ice cubes as well.

4. Blend the mixture until it becomes smooth and creamy.

5. Taste the smoothie and adjust the sweetness to your liking by adding more erythritol if needed.

6. Once the smoothie is well blended and sweetened to your preference, pour it into two glasses.

7. If desired, you can garnish the smoothie with a dusting of cocoa powder or a few chocolate shavings.

8. Serve the avocado and cocoa smoothie immediately and enjoy!

Nutritional Information (Per Serving):

- Carbs: 9g

- Phosphorus: 75mg

- Potassium: 400mg

- Sodium: 150mg

- Protein: 2g

Poached Pears with Cinnamon and Vanilla
Prep Time: 10 minutes
Cook Time: 25 minutes
Number of Servings: 4

Ingredients:

- 4 ripe pears (Bartlett or Anjou)

- 2 cups water

- 1/4 cup erythritol (sugar substitute)

- 2 cinnamon sticks

- 1 vanilla bean, split and scraped (or one teaspoon pure vanilla extract)
- 1/4 teaspoon salt
- Zest of 1 lemon

Instructions:

1. Peel the pears, leaving the stems intact. Cut a small slice from the bottom of each pear so that they can stand upright.

2. In a large saucepan, add the water, erythritol, cinnamon sticks, scraped vanilla bean seeds (or vanilla extract), salt, and lemon zest.

3. Place the saucepan over medium heat and bring the mixture to a simmer.

4. Carefully add the pears to the simmering liquid. Ensure that the pears are fully submerged in the liquid.

5. Reduce the heat to low, cover the saucepan, and let the pears simmer for approximately 20-25 minutes, or until tender. You can test their doneness by inserting a fork; it should go through easily.

6. Once the pears are poached, remove them from the liquid and place them in serving bowls.

7. If desired, you can reduce the poaching liquid by simmering it for an extra 10-15 minutes to create a syrupy sauce.

8. Drizzle the syrup over the poached pears.

9. Serve the poached pears with cinnamon and vanilla warm or at room temperature.

Nutritional Information (Per Serving):

- Carbs: 25g
- Phosphorus: 20mg
- Potassium: 210mg
- Sodium: 150mg
- Protein: 1g

Sugar-Free Chocolate Avocado Truffles

Prep Time: 20 minutes
Cook Time: 0 minutes
Number of Servings: 12 truffles

Ingredients:

- 2 ripe avocados

- 1/2 cup unsweetened cocoa powder

- 1/4 cup erythritol (sugar substitute)

- 1 teaspoon vanilla extract

- A pinch of salt

- 1/4 cup finely chopped unsalted almonds (for coating)

Instructions:

1. Cut the ripe avocados in half, take out the pits, and scoop the flesh into a mixing bowl.

2. Add the unsweetened cocoa powder, erythritol, vanilla extract, and a pinch of salt to the bowl with the avocado.

3. Mash and stir the mixture until it's smooth and all the ingredients are well combined.

4. Taste the mixture and adjust the sweetness to your liking by adding more erythritol if needed.

5. Once the mixture is well mixed and sweetened to your preference, place it in the refrigerator for about 15-20 minutes to firm up slightly.

6. While the mixture is chilling, prepare a plate or tray lined with parchment paper.

7. After the mixture has firmed up a bit, scoop out small portions and roll them into 12 equally-sized truffles, using your hands.

8. Roll each truffle in finely chopped unsalted almonds to coat them evenly.

9. Place the coated truffles on the parchment paper-lined plate or tray.

10. Refrigerate the truffles for an extra 15-20 minutes to set.

11. Once set, transfer the truffles to an airtight container for storage.

Nutritional Information (Per Serving - 1 Truffle):

- Carbs: 4g

- Phosphorus: 20mg

- Potassium: 150mg

- Sodium: 1mg

- Protein: 1g

Raspberry Chia Seed Parfait

Prep Time: 15 minutes
Cook Time: 0 minutes
Number of Servings: 2

Ingredients:

- 1 cup fresh raspberries

- 1 tablespoon erythritol (sugar substitute)

- 1 tablespoon chia seeds

- 1 cup unsweetened Greek yogurt

- 1/4 teaspoon vanilla extract

- 2 tablespoons chopped unsalted almonds

Instructions:

1. In a small bowl, mash the fresh raspberries with a fork and stir in the erythritol. Set this raspberry mixture aside.

2. In an extra bowl, add the chia seeds, unsweetened Greek yogurt, and vanilla extract. Mix them together and let the mixture sit for about 5 minutes to allow the chia seeds to absorb some of the liquid.

3. Take two serving glasses or bowls and start layering the parfait.

4. Begin with a layer of the chia seed and Greek yogurt mixture.

5. Add a layer of the raspberry mixture on top.

6. Continue alternating layers until you've used all of the mixtures, finishing with a layer of raspberries on top.

7. Sprinkle the chopped unsalted almonds evenly over the top of each parfait.

8. Refrigerate the parfaits for at least 30 minutes to allow the flavors to meld and the chia seeds to fully absorb the liquid.

9. Serve the raspberry chia seed parfaits chilled.

Nutritional Information (Per Serving):

- Carbs: 15g

- Phosphorus: 140mg

- Potassium: 240mg

- Sodium: 40mg

- Protein: 10g

Baked Pears with Cinnamon and Walnuts

Prep Time: 10 minutes
Cook Time: 30 minutes
Number of Servings: 4

Ingredients:

- 4 ripe pears (Bartlett or Anjou)

- 1/4 cup chopped unsalted walnuts

- 1 tablespoon erythritol (sugar substitute)

- 1/2 teaspoon ground cinnamon

- 1/4 teaspoon vanilla extract

- A pinch of salt

- 1/2 cup water

Instructions:

1. Turn on your oven and set it to 375°F (190°C).

2. Wash the pears and cut them in half lengthwise. Take out the cores and seeds with a spoon, creating a small well in each pear half.

3. In a small bowl, add the chopped unsalted walnuts, erythritol, ground cinnamon, vanilla extract, and a pinch of salt. Mix these ingredients together.

4. Fill each pear half with the walnut mixture, pressing it gently into the well you created.

5. Place the stuffed pear halves in a baking dish, cut side up.

6. Pour the water into the bottom of the baking dish.

7. Cover the baking dish with aluminum foil.

8. Bake the pears in the preheated oven for about 30 minutes or until tender when pierced with a fork.

9. Take out the foil and bake for an extra 5 minutes to allow the tops to brown slightly.

10. Once baked, take out the pears from the oven and let them cool slightly.

11. Serve the baked pears with cinnamon and walnuts warm or at room temperature.

Nutritional Information (Per Serving):

- Carbs: 20g
- Phosphorus: 75mg
- Potassium: 150mg
- Sodium: 5mg
- Protein: 1g

Pumpkin Spice Rice Pudding
Prep Time: 10 minutes
Cook Time: 30 minutes
Number of Servings: 4

Ingredients:

- 1 cup uncooked white rice
- 2 cups unsweetened almond milk
- 1 cup canned pumpkin puree
- 1/4 cup erythritol (sugar substitute)
- 1 teaspoon ground cinnamon
- 1/2 teaspoon ground nutmeg
- 1/4 teaspoon ground cloves
- 1/4 teaspoon ground ginger
- 1/4 teaspoon salt
- 1 teaspoon vanilla extract
- 2 tablespoons chopped unsalted almonds (for garnish, optional)

Instructions:

1. Rinse the uncooked white rice under cold water until the water runs clear.

2. In a large saucepan, add the rinsed rice and unsweetened almond milk. Bring the mixture to a boil over medium-high heat.

3. Once it boils, reduce the heat to low and let it simmer, uncovered, for about 20-25 minutes, or until the rice is tender and most of the liquid is absorbed. Stir occasionally to prevent sticking.

4. In a separate bowl, add the canned pumpkin puree, erythritol, ground cinnamon, ground nutmeg, ground cloves, ground ginger, salt, and vanilla extract.

5. When the rice is cooked, remove it from the heat and stir in the pumpkin spice mixture.

6. Return the saucepan to low heat and cook for an extra 5-10 minutes, stirring continuously until the mixture thickens to your desired consistency.

7. Once the rice pudding is ready, remove it from the heat and let it cool slightly.

8. If desired, garnish each serving with chopped unsalted almonds.

9. Serve the pumpkin spice rice pudding warm or at room temperature.

Nutritional Information (Per Serving):

- Carbs: 40g

- Phosphorus: 120mg

- Potassium: 200mg

- Sodium: 220mg

- Protein: 2g

Lemon Poppy Seed Coconut Flour Muffins

Prep Time: 15 minutes
Cook Time: 25 minutes
Number of Servings: 12 muffins

Ingredients:

- 1/2 cup coconut flour

- 1/4 cup erythritol (sugar substitute)

- 1/2 teaspoon baking powder

- 1/4 teaspoon salt

- 4 large eggs

- 1/4 cup unsalted butter, melted

- 1/4 cup unsweetened almond milk

- Zest of 2 lemons

- Juice of 1 lemon

- 1 teaspoon vanilla extract

- 2 tablespoons poppy seeds

Instructions:

1. Turn on your oven and set it to 350°F (175°C). Line a muffin tin with paper liners or grease it lightly.

2. In a mixing bowl, add the coconut flour, erythritol, baking powder, and salt. Mix these dry ingredients together.

3. In a separate bowl, whisk the eggs until well beaten.

4. Add the melted unsalted butter, unsweetened almond milk, lemon zest, lemon juice, and vanilla extract to the beaten eggs. Mix these wet ingredients together.

5. Pour the wet mixture into the dry mixture and stir until the batter is smooth and there are no lumps.

6. Gently fold in the poppy seeds into the batter.

7. Allow the batter to rest for a few minutes to let the coconut flour absorb some moisture. If the batter thickens too much, you can add a little more almond milk to reach a muffin batter consistency.

8. Spoon the batter evenly into the prepared muffin tin, filling each cup about 2/3 full.

9. Bake in the preheated oven for approximately 20-25 minutes, or until a toothpick inserted into the center of a muffin comes out clean.

10. Take out the muffins from the oven and let them cool in the muffin tin for a few minutes before transferring them to a wire rack to cool completely.

11. Once the muffins are completely cool, ready to be served.

Nutritional Information (Per Muffin):

- Carbs: 6g
- Phosphorus: 40mg
- Potassium: 40mg
- Sodium: 110mg
- Protein: 3g

Blueberry Oat Bars
Prep Time: 15 minutes
Cook Time: 35 minutes
Number of Servings: 12 bars

Ingredients:

- 1 1/2 cups old-fashioned rolled oats
- 1/2 cup whole wheat flour
- 1/2 cup almond flour
- 1/4 cup erythritol (sugar substitute)
- 1/4 teaspoon salt
- 1/2 teaspoon ground cinnamon
- 1/4 cup unsalted butter, melted
- 1/4 cup unsweetened applesauce
- 1 large egg
- 1 teaspoon vanilla extract
- 1 cup fresh blueberries
- Cooking spray (for greasing)

Instructions:

1. Turn on your oven and set it to 350°F (175°C). Grease an 8x8-inch baking pan with cooking spray.

2. In a mixing bowl, add the old-fashioned rolled oats, whole wheat flour, almond flour, erythritol, salt, and ground cinnamon. Mix these dry ingredients together.

3. In a separate bowl, whisk the melted unsalted butter, unsweetened applesauce, egg, and vanilla extract until well combined.

4. Pour the wet mixture into the bowl with the dry ingredients. Stir until all the ingredients are thoroughly incorporated.

5. Gently fold in the fresh blueberries.

6. Pour the mixture into the prepared baking pan and spread it out evenly.

7. Bake in the preheated oven for about 30-35 minutes, or until the top is golden brown and a toothpick inserted into the center comes out clean.

8. Take out the pan from the oven and let it cool in the pan for about 10 minutes.

9. After it has cooled slightly, cut the baked mixture into 12 bars.

10. Allow the bars to cool completely in the pan on a wire rack.

11. Once cool, the blueberry oat bars are ready to be enjoyed.

Nutritional Information (Per Bar):

- Carbs: 17g

- Phosphorus: 60mg

- Potassium: 70mg

- Sodium: 45mg

- Protein: 4g

Strawberry Coconut Ice Cream

Prep Time: 15 minutes
Cook Time: 0 minutes
Number of Servings: 4

Ingredients:

- 2 cups frozen strawberries

- 1 can (13.5-ounce) full-fat coconut milk

- 1/4 cup erythritol (sugar substitute)

- 1 teaspoon vanilla extract

- A pinch of salt

Instructions:

1. Place the frozen strawberries, full-fat coconut milk, erythritol, vanilla extract, and a pinch of salt into a blender.

2. Blend the mixture until it becomes smooth and creamy. You may need to stop and scrape down the sides of the blender as needed to ensure everything is well combined.

3. Taste the mixture and adjust the sweetness to your liking by adding more erythritol if needed.

4. Once the mixture is smooth and sweetened to your preference, transfer it to an airtight container.

5. Place the container in the freezer for at least 2-3 hours, or until the ice cream reaches your desired firmness.

6. Before serving, let the ice cream sit at room temperature for a few minutes to soften slightly for easier scooping.

7. Scoop the strawberry coconut ice cream into bowls or cones.

8. Enjoy your homemade strawberry coconut ice cream!

Nutritional Information (Per Serving):

- Carbs: 11g

- Phosphorus: 40mg

- Potassium: 220mg

- Sodium: 20mg

- Protein: 1g

BEVERAGES

Green Tea with Lemon and Mint

Prep Time: 5 minutes

Cook Time: 5 minutes

Servings: 2

Ingredients:

- 2 cups of water
- 2 green tea bags
- 2 slices of fresh lemon
- 10 fresh mint leaves
- 1 tablespoon of honey (optional, for sweetness)

Instructions:

1. In a saucepan, bring two cups of water to a boil.
2. Once the water is boiling, remove it from the heat and add 2 green tea bags. Let them steep for 3-5 minutes.
3. While the tea is steeping, rinse and chop 10 fresh mint leaves.
4. After steeping, take out the tea bags and discard them.
5. Add 2 slices of fresh lemon and the chopped mint leaves to the hot tea.
6. Allow the tea to cool slightly, then add one tablespoon of honey if desired, and stir sufficiently.
7. Pour the green tea with lemon and mint into two cups or glasses.
8. Serve hot and enjoy your diabetic renal-friendly green tea!

Nutritional Information (per serving):

- Carbs: 6 grams
- Phosphorus: 20 mg
- Potassium: 70 mg

- Sodium: 5 mg
- Protein: 0.5 grams

Watermelon and Basil Infused Water

Prep Time: 10 minutes

Cook Time: 0 minutes

Servings: 4

Ingredients:

- 4 cups of water
- 2 cups of diced watermelon
- 8 fresh basil leaves
- 1/2 lemon, sliced
- 1/2 teaspoon of stevia or an extra sugar substitute (optional, for sweetness)

Instructions:

1. In a large pitcher, add 4 cups of water.
2. Dice two cups of fresh watermelon into small pieces and add them to the pitcher.
3. Rinse 8 fresh basil leaves and tear them slightly to release their flavor. Add them to the pitcher.
4. Slice 1/2 lemon into thin rounds and add them to the watermelon and basil mixture.
5. If desired, add 1/2 teaspoon of stevia or an extra sugar substitute to sweeten the infused water. Adjust the sweetness to your preference.
6. Stir the ingredients gently to combine.
7. Place the pitcher in the refrigerator and let the flavors infuse for at least 1-2 hours before serving. For stronger flavors, you can refrigerate overnight.
8. Serve the refreshing watermelon and basil infused water over ice and enjoy.

Nutritional Information (per serving):

- Carbs: 5 grams
- Phosphorus: 10 mg
- Potassium: 60 mg
- Sodium: 0 mg
- Protein: 0.5 grams

Cucumber and Ginger Detox Water

Prep Time: 10 minutes

Cook Time: 0 minutes

Servings: 2

Ingredients:

- 4 cups of water
- 1 cucumber, thinly sliced
- 1-inch piece of fresh ginger, thinly sliced
- 1/2 lemon, thinly sliced
- 1/2 teaspoon of stevia or an extra sugar substitute (optional, for sweetness)

Instructions:

1. In a large pitcher, add 4 cups of water.
2. Thinly slice 1 cucumber and add the cucumber slices to the pitcher.
3. Thinly slice a 1-inch piece of fresh ginger and add it to the cucumber and water mixture.
4. Slice 1/2 lemon into thin rounds and also add them to the pitcher.
5. If desired, add 1/2 teaspoon of stevia or an extra sugar substitute to sweeten the detox water. Adjust the sweetness to your preference.
6. Stir the ingredients gently to combine.

7. Place the pitcher in the refrigerator and let the flavors infuse for at least 1-2 hours before serving. For stronger flavors, you can refrigerate overnight.

8. Serve the refreshing cucumber and ginger detox water over ice and enjoy.

Nutritional Information (per serving):

- Carbs: 3 grams

- Phosphorus: 10 mg

- Potassium: 70 mg

- Sodium: 5 mg

- Protein: 0.5 grams

Berry Blast Smoothie with Spinach

Prep Time: 5 minutes

Cook Time: 0 minutes

Servings: 2

Ingredients:

- 1 cup of fresh spinach leaves

- 1/2 cup of frozen mixed berries (strawberries, blueberries, raspberries)

- 1/2 banana

- 1 cup of unsweetened almond milk

- 1/2 cup of plain Greek yogurt

- 1 tablespoon of chia seeds

- 1/2 teaspoon of vanilla extract

- 1/2 teaspoon of stevia or an extra sugar substitute (optional, for sweetness)

Instructions:

1. Start by adding one cup of fresh spinach leaves to your blender.

2. Add 1/2 cup of frozen mixed berries (strawberries, blueberries, raspberries) to the blender.

3. Peel and add 1/2 banana to the blender as well.

4. Pour in one cup of unsweetened almond milk.

5. Add 1/2 cup of plain Greek yogurt to the other ingredients in the blender.

6. Sprinkle in one tablespoon of chia seeds for added fiber and omega-3s.

7. Add 1/2 teaspoon of vanilla extract to enhance the flavor.

8. If you desire a sweeter taste, include 1/2 teaspoon of stevia or an extra sugar substitute. Adjust the sweetness to your preference.

9. Blend all the ingredients until the smoothie is well mixed and has a creamy texture.

10. Pour the Berry Blast Smoothie into two glasses.

11. Serve immediately and enjoy!

Nutritional Information (per serving):

- Carbs: 20 grams
- Phosphorus: 110 mg
- Potassium: 300 mg
- Sodium: 80 mg
- Protein: 10 grams

Iced Hibiscus Tea with Stevia

Prep Time: 5 minutes

Cook Time: 10 minutes (plus cooling time)

Servings: 4

Ingredients:

- 4 cups of water
- 4 hibiscus tea bags

- 1/2 teaspoon of stevia or an extra sugar substitute

- 1/2 lemon, sliced (optional)

- Ice cubes (optional)

Instructions:

1. In a saucepan, bring 4 cups of water to a boil.

2. Once the water is boiling, remove it from the heat and add 4 hibiscus tea bags.

3. Allow the tea bags to steep in the hot water for 5-7 minutes to extract the flavor.

4. After steeping, take out the tea bags and discard them.

5. If you prefer a sweeter taste, add 1/2 teaspoon of stevia or an extra sugar substitute to the hot tea. Adjust the sweetness to your preference.

6. Optional: Add slices of 1/2 lemon to the tea for a citrusy twist.

7. Let the tea cool to room temperature, then refrigerate until it's chilled.

8. When you're ready to serve, fill glasses with ice cubes, if desired.

9. Pour the chilled hibiscus tea over the ice cubes or directly into glasses.

10. Garnish with lemon slices, if desired.

11. Serve your refreshing Iced Hibiscus Tea with Stevia and enjoy!

Nutritional Information (per serving):

- Carbs: 3 grams

- Phosphorus: 10 mg

- Potassium: 15 mg

- Sodium: 10 mg

- Protein: 0 grams

Almond Milk Latte with Cinnamon
Prep Time: 5 minutes

Cook Time: 5 minutes

Servings: 1

Ingredients:

- 1 cup of unsweetened almond milk
- 1 shot of espresso (approximately 1 ounce)
- 1/2 teaspoon of ground cinnamon
- 1/2 teaspoon of stevia or an extra sugar substitute (optional, for sweetness)
- Ground cinnamon for garnish (optional)

Instructions:

1. In a small saucepan, heat one cup of unsweetened almond milk over low to medium heat. Heat it until it's hot but not boiling, stirring occasionally. This should take about 3-5 minutes.

2. While the almond milk is heating, prepare 1 shot of espresso using an espresso machine or an extra preferred method.

3. Once the almond milk is hot, remove it from the heat and add 1/2 teaspoon of ground cinnamon. Stir sufficiently to combine the cinnamon with the almond milk.

4. If you prefer a sweeter latte, add 1/2 teaspoon of stevia or an extra sugar substitute to the almond milk and cinnamon mixture. Adjust the sweetness to your preference.

5. Pour the prepared shot of espresso into a mug.

6. Slowly pour the cinnamon-infused almond milk over the espresso in the mug, holding back the foam with a spoon if necessary.

7. Optional: Sprinkle a pinch of ground cinnamon on top of the latte for garnish and extra flavor.

8. Stir the latte gently to combine all the ingredients.

9. Serve your delicious Almond Milk Latte with Cinnamon immediately and enjoy!

Nutritional Information (per serving):

- Carbs: 1 gram

- Phosphorus: 40 mg

- Potassium: 160 mg

- Sodium: 160 mg

- Protein: 1 gram

Freshly Squeezed Orange and Carrot Juice

Prep Time: 10 minutes

Cook Time: 0 minutes

Servings: 2

Ingredients:

- 4 large carrots, peeled and chopped

- 4 large oranges, peeled and segmented

- 1/2 lemon, peeled and seeded

- 1/2 teaspoon of stevia or an extra sugar substitute (optional, for sweetness)

- Ice cubes (optional)

Instructions:

1. Begin by preparing the ingredients. Peel and chop 4 large carrots, peel and segment 4 large oranges, and peel and seed 1/2 lemon.

2. Place the chopped carrots, segmented oranges, and lemon into a high-speed blender.

3. If you prefer a sweeter juice, add 1/2 teaspoon of stevia or an extra sugar substitute to the blender. Adjust the sweetness to your preference.

4. Blend the ingredients on high until you achieve a smooth and well-mixed juice. This usually takes 1-2 minutes.

5. If you want a chilled juice, you can add a handful of ice cubes to the blender and blend again until the ice is crushed and the juice is cold.

6. Once the juice is ready, pour it through a fine-mesh strainer into a pitcher to remove any pulp and solids. Use the back of a spoon to press down on the solids to extract as much juice as possible.

7. Discard the remaining solids.

8. Pour the freshly squeezed Orange and Carrot Juice into glasses.

9. Optionally, add ice cubes to each glass for a colder drink.

10. Serve your refreshing juice immediately and enjoy!

Nutritional Information (per serving):

- Carbs: 30 grams

- Phosphorus: 100 mg

- Potassium: 700 mg

- Sodium: 80 mg

- Protein: 3 grams

Cranberry and Raspberry Sparkling Water

Prep Time: 5 minutes

Cook Time: 0 minutes

Servings: 2

Ingredients:

- 1 cup of unsweetened cranberry juice

- 1/2 cup of fresh raspberries

- 2 cups of sparkling water

- 1/2 lemon, thinly sliced

- 1/2 teaspoon of stevia or an extra sugar substitute (optional, for sweetness)

- Ice cubes (optional)

Instructions:

1. Start by pouring one cup of unsweetened cranberry juice into a pitcher.

2. Add 1/2 cup of fresh raspberries to the cranberry juice.

3. Thinly slice 1/2 lemon and add the lemon slices to the pitcher.

4. If you prefer a sweeter drink, add 1/2 teaspoon of stevia or an extra sugar substitute to the pitcher. Adjust the sweetness to your preference.

5. Pour two cups of sparkling water into the pitcher, gently stirring the ingredients to combine.

6. If you want a colder beverage, add ice cubes to the pitcher or directly to serving glasses.

7. Serve the Cranberry and Raspberry Sparkling Water in glasses filled with ice cubes, if desired.

8. Garnish with additional raspberries or lemon slices if you like.

9. Serve immediately and enjoy your refreshing drink!

Nutritional Information (per serving):

- Carbs: 15 grams
- Phosphorus: 15 mg
- Potassium: 50 mg
- Sodium: 15 mg
- Protein: 0.5 grams

Golden Milk (Turmeric) Latte

Prep Time: 5 minutes

Cook Time: 10 minutes

Servings: 2

Ingredients:

- 2 cups of unsweetened almond milk
- 1 teaspoon of ground turmeric
- 1/2 teaspoon of ground cinnamon
- 1/4 teaspoon of ground ginger

- 1/4 teaspoon of ground black pepper
- 1/2 teaspoon of vanilla extract
- 1/2 teaspoon of stevia or an extra sugar substitute (optional, for sweetness)

Instructions:

1. In a small saucepan, pour two cups of unsweetened almond milk.
2. Add one teaspoon of ground turmeric to the almond milk.
3. Mix in 1/2 teaspoon of ground cinnamon.
4. Incorporate 1/4 teaspoon of ground ginger.
5. Add 1/4 teaspoon of ground black pepper to enhance the absorption of turmeric.
6. Stir in 1/2 teaspoon of vanilla extract for flavor.
7. If you prefer a sweeter taste, add 1/2 teaspoon of stevia or an extra sugar substitute to the mixture. Adjust the sweetness to your preference.
8. Heat the mixture over low to medium heat, stirring constantly. Heat it until it's hot but not boiling. This should take about 5-7 minutes.
9. Once the Golden Milk Latte is hot and well-mixed, remove it from the heat.
10. Carefully pour the latte into two cups.
11. Serve your delicious and nutritious Golden Milk Latte immediately and enjoy!

Nutritional Information (per serving):

- Carbs: 3 grams
- Phosphorus: 40 mg
- Potassium: 160 mg
- Sodium: 160 mg
- Protein: 1 gram

Coconut Water with Lime and Mint

Prep Time: 5 minutes

Cook Time: 0 minutes

Servings: 2

Ingredients:

- 2 cups of unsweetened coconut water
- Juice of 1 lime
- 10 fresh mint leaves
- 1/2 teaspoon of stevia or an extra sugar substitute (optional, for sweetness)
- Ice cubes (optional)

Instructions:

1. In a pitcher, pour two cups of unsweetened coconut water.
2. Squeeze the juice of 1 lime into the coconut water.
3. Rinse and tear 10 fresh mint leaves slightly to release their flavor, then add them to the pitcher.
4. If you prefer a sweeter taste, add 1/2 teaspoon of stevia or an extra sugar substitute to the coconut water mixture. Adjust the sweetness to your preference.
5. Stir the ingredients gently to combine.
6. Optionally, add ice cubes to the pitcher or directly to serving glasses for a colder drink.
7. Serve your refreshing Coconut Water with Lime and Mint in glasses filled with ice cubes, if desired.
8. Garnish with a lime slice or additional mint leaves for extra freshness.
9. Serve immediately and enjoy!

Nutritional Information (per serving):

- Carbs: 10 grams
- Phosphorus: 70 mg

- Potassium: 500 mg
- Sodium: 50 mg
- Protein: 0 grams

Raspberry and Mint Infused Water

Prep Time: 5 minutes

Cook Time: 0 minutes

Servings: 2

Ingredients:

- 2 cups of water
- 1/2 cup of fresh raspberries
- 10 fresh mint leaves
- 1/2 lemon, thinly sliced
- Ice cubes (optional)

Instructions:

1. In a pitcher, pour two cups of water.
2. Add 1/2 cup of fresh raspberries to the water.
3. Rinse and tear 10 fresh mint leaves slightly to release their flavor, then add them to the pitcher.
4. Thinly slice 1/2 lemon and add the lemon slices to the infused water.
5. Optionally, add ice cubes to the pitcher or directly to serving glasses for a colder drink.
6. Stir the ingredients gently to combine.
7. Let the Raspberry and Mint Infused Water sit for at least 10 minutes to allow the flavors to meld.
8. Serve the refreshing infused water in glasses filled with ice cubes, if desired.

9. Garnish with extra raspberries, mint leaves, or lemon slices for added visual appeal.

10. Serve immediately and enjoy!

Nutritional Information (per serving):

- Carbs: 5 grams
- Phosphorus: 10 mg
- Potassium: 50 mg
- Sodium: 10 mg
- Protein: 0 grams

Ginger Turmeric Tea

Prep Time: 5 minutes

Cook Time: 10 minutes

Servings: 2

Ingredients:

- 2 cups of water
- 1-inch piece of fresh ginger, thinly sliced
- 1-inch piece of fresh turmeric, thinly sliced (or one teaspoon of ground turmeric)
- 1/2 teaspoon of ground black pepper
- 1/2 lemon, juiced
- 1/2 teaspoon of stevia or an extra sugar substitute (optional, for sweetness)

Instructions:

1. In a saucepan, bring two cups of water to a boil.

2. While the water is heating, thinly slice a 1-inch piece of fresh ginger and a 1-inch piece of fresh turmeric. If using ground turmeric, measure out 1 teaspoon.

3. Once the water is boiling, add the sliced ginger and turmeric (or ground turmeric) to the water.

4. Add 1/2 teaspoon of ground black pepper to the saucepan to enhance the absorption of turmeric.

5. Reduce the heat to low and simmer the mixture for 5-10 minutes. The longer you simmer, the stronger the flavors will be.

6. After simmering, take out the saucepan from the heat.

7. Strain the tea into two cups, using a fine-mesh strainer or a tea strainer to take out the ginger and turmeric slices or any remaining solids.

8. Squeeze the juice of 1/2 lemon into the tea for added flavor.

9. If you prefer a sweeter taste, add 1/2 teaspoon of stevia or an extra sugar substitute to the tea. Adjust the sweetness to your preference.

10. Stir sufficiently to combine all the ingredients.

11. Serve your Ginger Turmeric Tea immediately and enjoy the soothing and flavorful beverage!

Nutritional Information (per serving):

- Carbs: 4 grams
- Phosphorus: 20 mg
- Potassium: 120 mg
- Sodium: 10 mg
- Protein: 0.5 grams

Kiwi and Spinach Smoothie

Prep Time: 5 minutes

Cook Time: 0 minutes

Servings: 2

Ingredients:

- 2 ripe kiwis, peeled and sliced
- 1 cup of fresh spinach leaves
- 1/2 banana

- 1 cup of unsweetened almond milk

- 1/2 teaspoon of stevia or an extra sugar substitute (optional, for sweetness)

- Ice cubes (optional)

Instructions:

1. Start by preparing the ingredients. Peel and slice 2 ripe kiwis.

2. Measure out one cup of fresh spinach leaves.

3. Peel and slice 1/2 banana.

4. In a blender, add the sliced kiwis, fresh spinach leaves, and sliced banana.

5. Pour in one cup of unsweetened almond milk.

6. If you prefer a sweeter smoothie, add 1/2 teaspoon of stevia or an extra sugar substitute to the blender. Adjust the sweetness to your preference.

7. Optionally, add ice cubes to the blender for a colder drink.

8. Blend all the ingredients until you achieve a smooth and creamy texture. This usually takes 1-2 minutes.

9. Once the Kiwi and Spinach Smoothie is well-mixed, pour it into two glasses.

10. Serve your nutritious and delicious smoothie immediately and enjoy!

Nutritional Information (per serving):

- Carbs: 20 grams

- Phosphorus: 80 mg

- Potassium: 500 mg

- Sodium: 160 mg

- Protein: 3 grams

Cucumber and Basil Smoothie
Prep Time: 5 minutes

Cook Time: 0 minutes

Servings: 2

Ingredients:

- 2 cups of chopped cucumber (peeled if desired)
- 1/2 cup of fresh basil leaves
- 1 cup of unsweetened almond milk
- 1/2 lemon, juiced
- 1/2 teaspoon of stevia or an extra sugar substitute (optional, for sweetness)
- Ice cubes (optional)

Instructions:

1. Begin by preparing the ingredients. Chop two cups of cucumber, and if desired, peel the cucumber before chopping.
2. Rinse and prepare 1/2 cup of fresh basil leaves.
3. Juice 1/2 lemon to add a citrusy twist to the smoothie.
4. In a blender, add the chopped cucumber, fresh basil leaves, and lemon juice.
5. Pour in one cup of unsweetened almond milk.
6. If you prefer a sweeter smoothie, add 1/2 teaspoon of stevia or an extra sugar substitute to the blender. Adjust the sweetness to your preference.
7. Optionally, add ice cubes to the blender for a colder and more refreshing drink.
8. Blend all the ingredients until you achieve a smooth and creamy texture. This usually takes 1-2 minutes.
9. Once the Cucumber and Basil Smoothie is well-mixed, pour it into two glasses.
10. Serve your revitalizing and nutritious smoothie immediately and enjoy!

Nutritional Information (per serving):

- Carbs: 10 grams

- Phosphorus: 40 mg

- Potassium: 320 mg

- Sodium: 120 mg

- Protein: 2 grams

Almond Milk Matcha Latte

Prep Time: 5 minutes

Cook Time: 5 minutes

Servings: 2

Ingredients:

- 2 cups of unsweetened almond milk

- 2 teaspoons of matcha green tea powder

- 1/2 teaspoon of vanilla extract

- 1/2 teaspoon of stevia or an extra sugar substitute (optional, for sweetness)

Instructions:

1. In a small saucepan, pour two cups of unsweetened almond milk.

2. Heat the almond milk over low to medium heat, stirring occasionally. Heat it until it's hot but not boiling, which should take about 3-5 minutes.

3. While the almond milk is heating, measure out two teaspoons of matcha green tea powder.

4. In a separate small bowl, add the matcha powder with two tablespoons of hot water. Stir sufficiently until the matcha is fully dissolved to create a matcha paste.

5. Once the almond milk is hot, remove it from the heat and stir in the matcha paste, ensuring it's well-mixed.

6. Add 1/2 teaspoon of vanilla extract to the mixture for flavor.

7. If you prefer a sweeter latte, add 1/2 teaspoon of stevia or an extra sugar substitute. Adjust the sweetness to your preference.

8. Stir sufficiently to combine all the ingredients.

9. Pour your Almond Milk Matcha Latte into two cups.

10. Serve your delicious and energizing latte immediately and enjoy!

Nutritional Information (per serving):

- Carbs: 2 grams

- Phosphorus: 40 mg

- Potassium: 80 mg

- Sodium: 160 mg

- Protein: 1 gram

Hibiscus and Orange Blossom Iced Tea

Prep Time: 5 minutes

Cook Time: 10 minutes (plus cooling time)

Servings: 4

Ingredients:

- 4 cups of water

- 4 hibiscus tea bags

- 1/2 teaspoon of orange blossom water

- 1/2 lemon, thinly sliced

- 1/2 teaspoon of stevia or an extra sugar substitute (optional, for sweetness)

- Ice cubes (optional)

Instructions:

1. In a saucepan, bring 4 cups of water to a boil.

2. Once the water is boiling, remove it from the heat and add 4 hibiscus tea bags.

3. Allow the tea bags to steep in the hot water for 5-7 minutes to extract the flavor.

4. After steeping, take out the tea bags and discard them.

5. Stir in 1/2 teaspoon of orange blossom water to infuse the tea with a delightful floral aroma.

6. If you prefer a sweeter taste, add 1/2 teaspoon of stevia or an extra sugar substitute to the hot tea. Adjust the sweetness to your preference.

7. Thinly slice 1/2 lemon and add the lemon slices to the tea for a citrusy twist.

8. Let the tea cool to room temperature, then refrigerate until it's chilled.

9. When you're ready to serve, fill glasses with ice cubes, if desired.

10. Pour the chilled Hibiscus and Orange Blossom Iced Tea over the ice cubes or directly into glasses.

11. Serve your refreshing iced tea immediately and enjoy!

Nutritional Information (per serving):

- Carbs: 3 grams
- Phosphorus: 10 mg
- Potassium: 15 mg
- Sodium: 10 mg
- Protein: 0 grams

Pineapple and Ginger Detox Smoothie

Prep Time: 5 minutes

Cook Time: 0 minutes

Servings: 2

Ingredients:

- 2 cups of fresh pineapple chunks
- 1-inch piece of fresh ginger, peeled and sliced

- 1 cup of unsweetened almond milk

- Juice of 1/2 lemon

- 1/2 teaspoon of stevia or an extra sugar substitute (optional, for sweetness)

- Ice cubes (optional)

Instructions:

1. Begin by preparing the ingredients. Peel and slice a 1-inch piece of fresh ginger.

2. Measure out two cups of fresh pineapple chunks.

3. Juice 1/2 lemon to add a citrusy kick to the smoothie.

4. In a blender, add the fresh pineapple chunks and sliced ginger.

5. Pour in one cup of unsweetened almond milk.

6. Add the juice of 1/2 lemon for extra flavor.

7. If you prefer a sweeter smoothie, add 1/2 teaspoon of stevia or an extra sugar substitute to the blender. Adjust the sweetness to your preference.

8. Optionally, add ice cubes to the blender for a colder and more refreshing drink.

9. Blend all the ingredients until you achieve a smooth and creamy texture. This usually takes 1-2 minutes.

10. Once the Pineapple and Ginger Detox Smoothie is well-mixed, pour it into two glasses.

11. Serve your revitalizing and nutritious smoothie immediately and enjoy!

Nutritional Information (per serving):

- Carbs: 25 grams

- Phosphorus: 40 mg

- Potassium: 380 mg

- Sodium: 120 mg

Chapter 8

30-Day Meal Plan

Here's a 30-day meal plan consisting of breakfast, lunch, dinner, and snacks using the recipes available in this cookbook. As a reminder, you can adjust portion sizes and ingredients depending on your diet and preferences.

Week 1
Day 1
- Breakfast: Spinach and Feta Egg White Omelet
- Lunch: Lentil and Vegetable Soup
- Dinner: Baked Salmon with Lemon and Dill
- Snack: Almond and Berry Protein Bites

Day 2
- Breakfast: Quinoa Porridge with Blueberries
- Lunch: Grilled Chicken Salad with Avocado and Lime Vinaigrette
- Dinner: Grilled Tofu and Asparagus with Tahini Sauce
- Snack: Roasted Edamame with Sea Salt

Day 3
- Breakfast: Scrambled Tofu with Tomatoes and Herbs
- Lunch: Tuna Salad Lettuce Wraps
- Dinner: Chicken and Vegetable Stir-Fry with Brown Rice
- Snack: Cottage Cheese with Pineapple

Day 4

- Breakfast: Greek Yogurt Parfait with Almonds and Berries
- Lunch: Spinach and Strawberry Salad with Balsamic Glaze
- Dinner: Eggplant and Chickpea Tagine
- Snack: Carrot and Cucumber Sticks with Hummus

Day 5

- Breakfast: Veggie and Cheese Breakfast Burrito
- Lunch: Cauliflower and Broccoli Rice Bowl with Grilled Shrimp
- Dinner: Spaghetti Squash with Turkey Bolognese
- Snack: Greek Yogurt with Honey and Walnuts

Day 6

- Breakfast: Zucchini and Mushroom Frittata
- Lunch: Turkey and Veggie Lettuce Wraps
- Dinner: Cod with Tomato and Olive Tapenade
- Snack: Baked Sweet Potato Fries

Day 7

- Breakfast: Cinnamon Raisin Oatmeal with Chia Seeds
- Lunch: Quinoa and Black Bean Stuffed Bell Peppers
- Dinner: Quinoa and Kale Stuffed Peppers
- Snack: Avocado Slices with Lime and Chili

Week 2
Day 8

- Breakfast: Smoked Salmon and Cream Cheese Wrap
- Lunch: Chickpea and Spinach Curry
- Dinner: Teriyaki Glazed Tempeh with Broccoli

- Snack: Popcorn Seasoned with Herbs and Nutritional Yeast

Day 9

- Breakfast: Sweet Potato and Black Bean Breakfast Bowl
- Lunch: Cucumber and Dill Tuna Salad
- Dinner: Ratatouille with Herbed Quinoa
- Snack: Pickle Spears Wrapped in Deli Turkey

Day 10

- Breakfast: Cottage Cheese Pancakes with Fresh Fruit
- Lunch: Roasted Vegetable and Barley Salad
- Dinner: Baked Cod with Herbed Quinoa
- Snack: Cucumber and Greek Yogurt Dip

Day 11

- Breakfast: Cinnamon Apple Quinoa Breakfast Bowl
- Lunch: Roasted Beet and Walnut Salad
- Dinner: Chicken and Asparagus Foil Packets
- Snack: Roasted Red Pepper and Walnut Hummus

Day 12

- Breakfast: Smoked Salmon and Avocado Breakfast Wrap
- Lunch: Lemon Garlic Shrimp and Asparagus
- Dinner: Spaghetti Squash Primavera
- Snack: Cherry Tomato and Mozzarella Skewers

Day 13

- Breakfast: Spinach and Mushroom Breakfast Casserole
- Lunch: Mediterranean Chickpea Salad
- Dinner: Vegan Lentil Shepherd's Pie
- Snack: Almond and Coconut Energy Balls

Day 14

- Breakfast: Blueberry Almond Chia Pudding
- Lunch: Broccoli and Cheddar Stuffed Sweet Potato
- Dinner: Lemon Dill Baked Tilapia
- Snack: Cottage Cheese with Sliced Peaches

Week 3

Day 15

- Breakfast: Veggie Breakfast Quesadilla
- Lunch: Turkey and Spinach Stuffed Mushrooms
- Dinner: Stuffed Portobello Mushrooms with Spinach and Feta
- Snack: Roasted Brussels Sprouts Chips

Day 16

- Breakfast: Tofu Scramble with Sun-Dried Tomatoes
- Lunch: Grilled Eggplant and Red Pepper Wrap
- Dinner: Cod with Tomato and Olive Tapenade
- Snack: Carrot and Zucchini Fritters

Day 17

- Breakfast: Peanut Butter and Banana Overnight Oats
- Lunch: Quinoa and Black Bean Salad with Lime Vinaigrette
- Dinner: Baked Salmon with Lemon and Dill
- Snack: Almond and Berry Protein Bites

Day 18

- Breakfast: Spinach and Feta Egg White Omelet
- Lunch: Lentil and Vegetable Soup
- Dinner: Grilled Tofu and Asparagus with Tahini Sauce

- Snack: Roasted Edamame with Sea Salt

Day 19

- Breakfast: Quinoa Porridge with Blueberries
- Lunch: Tuna Salad Lettuce Wraps
- Dinner: Chicken and Vegetable Stir-Fry with Brown Rice
- Snack: Cottage Cheese with Pineapple

Day 20

- Breakfast: Scrambled Tofu with Tomatoes and Herbs
- Lunch: Spinach and Strawberry Salad with Balsamic Glaze
- Dinner: Eggplant and Chickpea Tagine
- Snack: Carrot and Cucumber Sticks with Hummus

Day 21

- Breakfast: Greek Yogurt Parfait with Almonds and Berries
- Lunch: Turkey and Veggie Lettuce Wraps
- Dinner: Spaghetti Squash with Turkey Bolognese
- Snack: Greek Yogurt with Honey and Walnuts

Week 4
Day 22

- Breakfast: Veggie and Cheese Breakfast Burrito
- Lunch: Cauliflower and Broccoli Rice Bowl with Grilled Shrimp
- Dinner: Cod with Tomato and Olive Tapenade
- Snack: Baked Sweet Potato Fries

Day 23

- Breakfast: Zucchini and Mushroom Frittata

- Lunch: Chickpea and Spinach Curry
- Dinner: Teriyaki Glazed Tempeh with Broccoli
- Snack: Popcorn Seasoned with Herbs and Nutritional Yeast

Day 24

- Breakfast: Cinnamon Raisin Oatmeal with Chia Seeds
- Lunch: Quinoa and Black Bean Stuffed Bell Peppers
- Dinner: Ratatouille with Herbed Quinoa
- Snack: Avocado Slices with Lime and Chili

Day 25

- Breakfast: Sweet Potato and Black Bean Breakfast Bowl
- Lunch: Cucumber and Dill Tuna Salad
- Dinner: Baked Cod with Herbed Quinoa
- Snack: Pickle Spears Wrapped in Deli Turkey

Day 26

- Breakfast: Cottage Cheese Pancakes with Fresh Fruit
- Lunch: Roasted Vegetable and Barley Salad
- Dinner: Chicken and Asparagus Foil Packets
- Snack: Roasted Red Pepper and Walnut Hummus

Day 27

- Breakfast: Cinnamon Apple Quinoa Breakfast Bowl
- Lunch: Roasted Beet and Walnut Salad
- Dinner: Spaghetti Squash Primavera
- Snack: Cherry Tomato and Mozzarella Skewers

Day 28

- Breakfast: Smoked Salmon and Avocado Breakfast Wrap
- Lunch: Lemon Garlic Shrimp and Asparagus

- Dinner: Vegan Lentil Shepherd's Pie
- Snack: Almond and Coconut Energy Balls

Day 29

- Breakfast: Spinach and Mushroom Breakfast Casserole
- Lunch: Mediterranean Chickpea Salad
- Dinner: Lemon Dill Baked Tilapia
- Snack: Cottage Cheese with Sliced Peaches

Day 30

- Breakfast: Blueberry Almond Chia Pudding
- Lunch: Broccoli and Cheddar Stuffed Sweet Potato
- Dinner: Stuffed Portobello Mushrooms with Spinach and Feta
- Snack: Roasted Brussels Sprouts Chips

Chapter 9

Creating Balanced Diabetic Renal Meals

Creating well-balanced meals tailored to a diabetic renal diet is essential for individuals managing both diabetes and kidney disease. This chapter, "Building Balanced Diabetic Renal Meals," provides practical guidance for creating nutritious and tasty meals that meet the dietary requirements of individuals with diabetes and kidney disease. By incorporating a balanced approach to meal preparation, you can enjoy a diverse range of satisfying foods while also prioritizing your health.

Portion control and serving sizes

Managing a diabetic renal diet involves focusing on portion control. Understanding the correct serving sizes is essential for you to manage your calorie intake. This is crucial for controlling blood sugar levels and preventing weight gain, both of which can potentially lead to kidney problems. Here are some key principles to consider when it comes to portion control:

• **Measuring and Weighing**: Utilizing measuring cups, a kitchen scale, or even everyday objects (such as a deck of cards for meat portions) can offer a visual reference for accurate serving sizes.

• **Balanced Plates**: A balanced meal includes the right proportions of protein, carbohydrates, and vegetables. Dividing your plate into sections can help ensure balance.

• **Mindful Eating**: Being aware of hunger and fullness cues can help prevent overeating. Eating slowly and savoring each bite helps the body recognize fullness, which can reduce the urge to overeat.

• **Personalized Portions**: Serving sizes may vary based on factors such as age, gender, activity level, and specific health requirements. Consulting with a healthcare provider or dietitian is essential for determining appropriate portions.

Weekly meal planning

Meal planning is a crucial tool for managing a diabetic renal diet. It enables you to control the content and quality of your meals, ensuring that you can meet your dietary needs while still enjoying tasty food. Here are some tips for approaching weekly meal planning:

• **Variety is essential:** Plan a wide range of meals to avoid boredom. Including a variety of foods in your meals not only makes them more interesting, but also helps you consume a broader range of nutrients.

• **Consider Dietary Restrictions:** Customize meal plans to accommodate specific dietary restrictions or preferences. Whether it's vegetarian, vegan, or specific food allergies, there are various ways to modify recipes.

• **Preparation is Key:** Create a shopping list to make grocery trips more efficient and ensure you have a stock of kidney-friendly ingredients available. To make meal preparation more efficient, it is helpful to prepare ingredients in advance. This can include tasks such as chopping vegetables or marinating proteins.

• **Balance Your Diet Across Days:** While individual meals should be balanced, it's also vital to maintain a balanced diet throughout the week. If one meal contains a slightly higher amount of a specific nutrient, adjust the other meals to maintain overall balance.

Tips for Successful Grocery Shopping

Making wise choices at the grocery store is essential in building balanced meals for individuals with diabetic renal conditions. The shopping list should align with the planned meals and dietary requirements. Consider these tips for a successful grocery shopping experience:

• **Read Labels:** Pay attention to food labels, specifically looking for sodium, potassium, and phosphorus content. Choose products that have lower levels of these minerals.

• **Opt for Fresh Produce:** Fresh fruits and vegetables are great options. However, if you choose canned or frozen options, make sure to select those that do not have added salt or sugars.

• **Choose Lean Proteins**: Opt for lean cuts of meat, poultry, and fish, as they are excellent protein sources. It is advisable to limit the consumption of processed meats and marinated proteins that have high sodium content.

• **Shop the Perimeter**: Grocery stores often place fresh, unprocessed foods around the store's perimeter. Focus your shopping there to minimize exposure to unhealthy, processed foods in the center aisles.

• **Consider Meal Replacements**: Kidney-friendly meal replacement options can be convenient for quick and balanced meals. Consult with a healthcare professional to explore appropriate choices.

By carefully planning meals, controlling portion sizes, and making thoughtful choices at the grocery store, you can learn how to create balanced meals suitable for managing diabetes and renal conditions. Endeavor to make informed choices about your diet, so that every meal meets your health needs and satisfies your taste preferences. Once acquired, this skill can significantly improve your health and well-being.

Chapter 10

Managing Diabetic Kidney Health

This critical section of this cookbook thoroughly examines the different factors involved in maintaining kidney function while effectively managing diabetes. By exploring these key points, you can enhance your understanding of how to protect your kidneys and maintain your overall health.

Taking Medication and Regularly Monitoring Your Health.

1. Medication Regimen: Managing diabetes and kidney health often requires a careful approach to medication. This chapter discusses the common medications prescribed for individuals with both conditions, including oral antidiabetic drugs, insulin, and medications that help protect kidney function.

2. Blood Glucose Monitoring: Blood glucose monitoring is an essential part of managing diabetes. You should always monitor your blood sugar levels, select an appropriate glucose meter, and interpret the results to make necessary adjustments to your treatment plans.

3. Blood Pressure Regulation: Hypertension is a common comorbidity of diabetes and kidney disease, which can affect blood pressure control. Through your physician, you can get prescriptions for blood pressure medications. You should also monitor your blood pressure regularly and make the needed lifestyle adjustments to control hypertension.

4. Self-Care and Adherence: Managing a complex medical condition like diabetes and kidney disease often involves a significant amount of self-care and adherence to treatment plans. Try to care for yourself as much as you can and adhere to treatment plans for the best results.

Exercise and lifestyle choices

1. Importance of Physical Activity: Physical activity is critical for managing both diabetes and kidney health. Engaging in regular physical activity has various advantages, such as better blood sugar regulation, weight control, and improved cardiovascular well-being.

2. Exercise Guidelines: Discover practical guidelines for incorporating safe and effective exercise into your routine. You can engage in different types of physical activity, including aerobic exercises and strength training. Additionally, find ways to customize your workouts based on your individual fitness level.

3. Lifestyle Modifications: Making lifestyle changes, such as quitting smoking and reducing alcohol intake, positively affects kidney health. Explore strategies for adopting a kidney-friendly lifestyle and reducing risk factors associated with both conditions.

4. Stress Management: Chronic stress can have a negative impact on blood sugar levels and overall well-being. Stress management techniques such as mindfulness, meditation, and relaxation exercises help to put your mind and body at ease, thereby relieving stress.

Staying motivated and well-informed

1. Setting Achievable Goals: Achieving and maintaining health goals can be challenging, but it's essential for long-term success. To ensure success with this diabetic-friendly renal diet cookbook, set achievable and realistic goals for managing your diabetes and kidney health.

2. Support Systems: Support systems play a significant role in making all human endeavors either succeed or fail. Friends, family, and healthcare providers can play a role in fostering motivation and accountability. Search for and join support groups online with like-minded people to connect with others facing similar challenges.

3. Staying Informed: Diabetes and kidney disease management is constantly changing. Read up and stay informed about the latest research, treatment options, and dietary recommendations in order to adjust your strategies accordingly.

4. Stay Positive: Some challenges may arise while managing diabetes and kidney health. Maintaining a positive outlook empowers you in your journey towards better health.

By understanding the role of medication, making healthy lifestyle choices, and staying motivated and informed, you can take control of your health and lead a fulfilling life while effectively managing these health conditions.

Conclusion

As we near the end of this exploration of diabetic renal diets, it is only necessary that you reflect on your progress and recommit to your health and well-being. This final section emphasizes the significance of balance, nourishment, and perseverance in managing diabetes and kidney disease. Here is a summary of the main points that provide valuable insights you can apply.

Your Path to Better Health

1. Celebrating Success: It's essential to recognize and acknowledge the progress you've made in adopting a diabetic renal diet and living a healthy lifestyle. This will help you stay motivated.

2. The Power of Resilience: Resilience is a potent quality that helps us overcome challenges in life. It becomes especially important when dealing with chronic health conditions such as diabetes and kidney disease, which can be quite demanding to manage. Try being resilient, as occasional mistakes should not discourage you from making progress.

3. A Holistic Approach: Always consider your health holistically. Health is not solely defined by the absence of disease, but also encompasses the presence of physical, mental, and emotional well-being. It is necessary to address all health aspects for a truly fulfilling life.

Embracing Delicious and Nutritious Eating

1. The Pleasure of Food: A diabetic renal diet is not solely focused on deprivation, but instead on making mindful choices to savor the joy of eating. This dietary path allows for the enjoyment of delicious and nutritious meals.

2. Exploring Creativity in the Kitchen: Continue your culinary curiosity beyond this cookbook. Try out new recipes, discover those that work for you, and broaden your culinary horizons. The world of healthy and delicious food is vast and full of possibilities.

3. Sharing the Knowledge: Share your knowledge and culinary creations with loved ones and create a support network of health-conscious individuals who can embark on this journey together.

By embracing the principles of balance, nourishment, and resilience, you will become empowered to make choices that contribute to a healthier and more vibrant life. Here's to a brighter, more nutritious, and more flavorful future than ever before.

Recipe Index

Roasted Brussels Sprouts Chips 92

Roasted Edamame with Sea Salt 76

Roasted Red Pepper and Walnut Hummus 87

Roasted Vegetable and Barley Salad 40

S

Scrambled Tofu with Tomatoes and Herbs 7

Smoked Salmon and Avocado Breakfast Wrap 19

Smoked Salmon and Cream Cheese Wrap 14

Spaghetti Squash Primavera 68

Spaghetti Squash with Turkey Bolognese 57

Spinach and Feta Egg White Omelet 5

Spinach and Mushroom Breakfast Casserole 20

Spinach and Strawberry Salad with Balsamic Glaze 32

Strawberry Coconut Ice Cream 115

Stuffed Portobello Mushrooms with Spinach and Feta 73

Sugar-Free Chocolate Avocado Truffles 107

Sugar-Free Mixed Berry Sorbet 95

Sweet Potato and Black Bean Breakfast Bowl 15

T

Teriyaki Glazed Tempeh with Broccoli 62

Tofu Scramble with Sun-Dried Tomatoes 25

Tuna Salad Lettuce Wraps 30

Turkey and Spinach Meatballs in Tomato Sauce 63

Turkey and Spinach Stuffed Mushrooms 47

Turkey and Veggie Lettuce Wraps 34

V

Vegan Lentil Shepherd's Pie 70

Veggie and Cheese Breakfast Burrito 10

Veggie Breakfast Quesadilla 23

W

Watermelon and Basil Infused Water 118

Z

Zucchini and Mushroom Frittata 11

Made in United States
Orlando, FL
09 April 2025

60319562R00090